About the Author

Appointed Travel Correspondent by *The Times* in 1967 (the first in the paper's history), John Carter became one of the UK's best-known travel journalists and presenters, broadcasting for nearly thirty years on programmes such as the BBC's *Holiday* programme – a series he helped create – and then ITV's *Wish You Were Here...?* He has travelled the world for over half a century on behalf of newspapers, magazines, radio and television programmes in a professional life that has been crammed with incidents and encounters, many of which never made it to the printed page or television screen. Now, for the first time, he has set some of those stories down on paper.

Gullible's Travels ✈

Confessions of an International Towel Thief

Travel safely

John Carter

John Carter

Bradt

First published in the UK in July 2016 by

Bradt Travel Guides Ltd
IDC House, The Vale, Chalfont St Peter, Bucks SL9 9RZ, England
www.bradtguides.com

Print edition published in the USA by The Globe Pequot Press Inc,
PO Box 480, Guilford, Connecticut 06437-0480

Text copyright © 2016 John Carter
Photographs copyright © 2016 John Carter
Edited by Jennifer Barclay
Proofread by Janet Mears
Designed and typeset from the author's files by Ian Spick
Cover design by Ian Spick
Cover photographs by John Carter
Production managed by Sue Cooper, Bradt & Jellyfish Print Solutions

ISBN: 978 1 78477 032 7 (print)
e-ISBN: 978 1 78477 187 4 (e-pub)
e-ISBN: 978 1 78477 287 1 (mobi)

British Library Cataloguing in Publication Data
A catalogue record for this book is available from the British Library

Printed in the UK
Digital conversion by www.dataworks.co.in

Contents

Foreword

Early in my writing career, I was told by a veteran hack that, to qualify as a *bona fide* 'traveller's tale', an anecdote must be 100 per cent true – and 99 per cent unbelievable.

That, in a sentence, defines this collection. These stories are all completely true. There is, however, a small twist, which needs explaining.

Though the stories are drawn from my experiences during more than half a century of international travel, I have also included in this collection several 'factions' – that is, taking a situation from real life but tweaking it a little, to provide the sort of tidy conclusion that real life usually overlooks. They will be clearly signposted, as I do not intend to pull the wool over your eyes; all the factions here occurred on cruise ships, and were originally published in *Cruise* magazine. They should be read on the understanding that names and details have been changed to protect the innocent – not to mention the guilty.

'Factions' apart, the stories that follow are 100 per cent true. If you choose not to believe them, that is your prerogative.

That said, I do have a confession to make.

Don't be too concerned, I haven't committed a really big crime of the kind that is admitted at the end of television detective programmes – when all the participants are gathered in the drawing room, and shortly after one of them says: 'Good grief, Inspector, you don't mean to say the murderer is *one of us*?' No, nothing like that.

My confession is that I have forgotten some of the details. The stories are true, but I can't always recall exactly when they happened or the names of the people who were there at the time.

Historically, it has been fairly easy to pull the wool over people's eyes when it comes to the relating of travellers' tales. Marco Polo, who was something of a boyhood hero to me, is a good example.

I remember seeing a film about him one Saturday morning when I was around eleven – with Gary Cooper horribly miscast in the title role – and deciding that, when I grew up, I would have similar adventures and, with luck, meet the kind of pretty ladies who graced the court of Kublai Khan – at least, the version of his court that Hollywood depicted. This led to a long-distance, and unrequited, love affair with film star Yvonne De Carlo, but we won't go into that now...

In due course I bought and read *Travels*, Marco Polo's detailed account of his journeys, and what passed for his adventures. It was the most boring book I have ever ploughed through. I couldn't fathom why he hadn't dwelt on unusual stuff like the fact that people ate with little sticks instead of knives and spoons, or had invented kites which could carry a grown man high into the air – or gunpowder! Instead he went on for page after page about how many horses were owned by this, that or the other local lord, and similar uninteresting stuff.

All of which adds weight to the theory that Marco Polo never made that epic journey; that he travelled as far as the Black Sea port of Constanta, in present-day Romania, and wrote down the tales told by returning sailors.

I promise I haven't done that.

So, with seat belts securely fastened, seats in the upright position and tray tables folded away, let's get this journey started...

Adrenalin Rush

A couple of minutes before seven o'clock on the morning of 8th July in the early days of my career, I stood at the western end of the Calle de la Estafeta in Pamplona, wishing to God that I was somewhere else.

Anywhere else would do.

I was waiting for a flare to signal that the first of half a dozen bulls had been released from the pen less than 200 yards away. Calle de la Estafeta was part of the route to the bull ring. Waiting, I reflected on how I came to be in this hazardous situation.

✈

About a month earlier, over dinner in a restaurant somewhere in Devon, Tom Savage, the producer of the BBC's *Holiday* programme, had suggested that the San Fermín Festival in Pamplona – more usually known as the Bull Running – would make 'good television'. I agreed, but said it would make even better television if I wasn't a part of it. This comment was made from the heart as, apart from a tendency towards cowardice, I possess a well-honed sense of self-preservation.

Having grown up in close proximity to the countryside, I have seen what even a moderately annoyed cow can do to an innocent member of the human race. Dammit, I knew a farmer who had been badly injured by a bunch of sheep with no sense of direction. So I was not going to deliberately place myself in the path of a speeding bull. On this, my mind was firmly made up.

However, as the evening wore on I succumbed to that deadly combination of alcohol and stupidity that has been my undoing on so many occasions. I heard myself saying: 'Wow, what a great idea. Let's go for it.'

And so here I was, taking part in the ritual of the running of the bulls. And probably about to die as a result.

✈

I had no time to dwell further on my folly for the flare soared into the sky, followed a split second later by another. That was not a good sign, as it meant that the last of the bulls had left the corral. With hardly any time between first and last, those bulls were already coming at a hell of a pace. It was time to run.

We tried, the rest of the crowd and I, but a line of *Guardia Civil* blocked the way. Their orders were to prevent us stampeding and trampling on runners farther down the route. It was a sensible precaution, but not one we appreciated at the time. After what seemed like an age, but was no more than a few seconds, they moved aside and, sobbing with relief and fear, I ran like a terrified rabbit. Knowing I was in more danger from fellow runners than from the bulls was of little consolation, because the bulls didn't know this. Neither did the steers.

Now, nobody ever mentions the steers when they write about the thrills and excitement of Pamplona's bull-running festival. But half a dozen of those great, slab-sided creatures are released to run with the bulls, in theory as a calming influence – though how a castrated bull can be a calming influence on an uncastrated one, I have no idea; unless they were there to warn: 'If you don't behave yourself you'll end up like us.' Which is ridiculous when you realise that the uncastrated lads were all going to be dead by teatime. Anyway, steers are not supposed to present any danger, but as they are the fighting weight of a Vauxhall Astra, the slightest accidental nudge can do serious damage to your rib cage.

So I ran as fast as I could, thinking of horns and hooves and slight nudges and of how all that mobile beef was gaining on me. I ran in my stupid black beret and my ridiculous red scarf and my brand new espadrilles, because Tom had insisted we should all dress the part. I was determined not to die in such an outlandish outfit.

By a miracle, whimpering with terror, I made it to the bull ring and scrambled behind the wooden barrier. I lay on the seats, shuddering and sobbing, in the foetal position.

Now any day that has its adrenalin peak at 7.15 a.m. requires a large quantity of alcohol to get you to the end of it. And as the wine takes effect, you forget the fear and begin to believe you are Ernest Hemingway reincarnated. You lie about your bravery and the extent of the danger you had faced. This is mainly done to impress young ladies, who are supposed to gaze at you in doe-eyed admiration. Never has the term 'bullshitting' been so apt.

All that wine combined with bravado ensures that when, towards the end of the evening, somebody suggests you run again tomorrow (as some idiot invariably does), you hear a voice saying: 'Wow, what a great idea. Let's go for it.' And then you realise it is yours.

So, for four days I ran with the bulls. And by the fourth morning I had almost convinced myself I knew what I was doing. Almost.

However, that morning, there was a complication.

As I stood once more in Calle de la Estafeta, waiting for the signal flare, an English voice yelled out: 'Hello, old son. Fancy seeing you here. How the devil are you?'

I turned and immediately recognised the actor Trevor Howard. Clearly, he had mistaken me for someone he knew, for we had never met until that moment.

That wasn't the problem, however. The problem was that Mr Howard was absolutely blotto, as drunk as the proverbial skunk. He and a bunch of other folk had been driven through the night from the film festival in nearby San Sebastián, fortifying themselves with copious amounts of wine and, in Mr Howard's case, much brandy, too.

To this day I do not know who he thought I was. There was no way of finding out at the time, much less convincing him of his error. He had no idea where he was or what was about to happen, and was in the middle of one of those endless, pointless monologues much favoured by drunken people when the flare went up.

I turned to go. Mr Howard was in full flow and thought I was being rude. He said so, loudly and in picturesque language. He also grabbed me firmly by the shoulder so I would remain and listen to the conclusion of his lecture.

As people ran past us I saw, out of the corner of my eye, that the first of the bulls had entered the street. I pulled free from Mr Howard, who staggered back, shook his head, grunted and collapsed backwards like a broken puppet into a shop doorway where he promptly passed out. Pausing only to kick his legs into the safety of the doorway, I joined the fleeing mob. I made it to the bull ring, somehow overtaken *en route* by three bulls and four steers.

Though bull-running is the heart and soul of the San Fermín festival, there are also bull fights in Pamplona, but they are not very good. Their daily purpose is to dispose of the animals that made the morning run, but the fighters are either veterans on their way down or novices on their way up. But we had to film the bull fights, if for no other reason than to bring the wrath of anti-bullfighting viewers down on our heads. So, one hot afternoon, we took ourselves to the bull ring to do just that. Among the crowd was a group supporting one of the novice fighters who, for reasons known only to themselves, had brought along a duck as a mascot – a real duck.

From time to time this wretched bird was flung into the air, but could not get far as she had a long string attached to one of her legs and would be hauled back, quacking and flapping like an ungainly feathered kite. The spectacle was very cruel, and rather sad. We filmed it though we knew it could not be used, even if the duck gang had refrained from making extremely rude gestures towards us and our camera.

At the end of our last, long evening, on the way back to the hotel we encountered about a dozen of those fans, led by a burly bloke with a stubbled chin and a serious personal hygiene problem. He had a large plastic barrel of wine slung over one shoulder, and the semi-comatose duck stuffed into the top of his leather jacket.

Recognising us from our encounter in the arena, he barred our way, insisting we should drink wine with him and his chums. One of them had a load of thick green glass tumblers in a plastic bag, but Mr Stubble was hampered in his efforts to fill them from his barrel because of the duck. So he removed her from his jacket and placed her on the pavement.

Then the toasts started. To Pamplona! To Spain! To England! To Her Majesty Queen Elizabeth! To General Franco! (This was, as I mentioned, a long time ago…)

As we were in the process of swearing our undying love for each other, not to mention 'The Great English Broadcasting Company', the duck began to recover her senses. She had had a terrible day – indeed, a terrible week – and was in the mood for revenge.

My feet were inches from her head. She lunged at my bare ankle, ripping down with the serrated edge of her beak, drawing copious amounts of blood.

I dropped my tumbler – which, oddly, did not break but bounced several times along the roadway – and began to hop around in considerable pain. I also tried to kick the duck, but it is not possible to hop and kick at the same time. I may have sworn. I know Mr Stubble did, as he scooped up his duck, yelling abuse at me for trying to harm her, as he led his chums away. As the Victorian music hall ballad puts it: 'We parted on fighting terms.'

With the red scarf bound round my ankle as a makeshift bandage I limped back to the hotel, helped by my companions. Prue, our Production Assistant, cleaned up the wound, declared it did not need stitching and dressed it with a couple of large plasters from her BBC first aid kit.

Thus my Pamplona adventure came to an ignominious end. But it gave me a unique claim to fame.

I am the only person you'll ever meet who survived the bulls of Pamplona.

Only to be gored by a duck.

Algarve Interlude

After I began my travel writing career in 1961, I spent several months finding my feet and, literally, finding my way about. Accepting an assortment of invitations, I went on fact-finding press trips, getting to know my fellow scribes and gradually being accepted into the brotherhood (and, of course, the sisterhood) of travel writers.

I also tried to unlock the mysteries of the UK travel industry, meeting its leading lights, attempting to work out the difference between a travel agent and a tour operator and to understand the convoluted politics of different trade bodies – and more or less failing.

Then a chap named Ray Colegate, a civil servant with the Civil Aviation Authority, sorted it out for me in a single sentence.

'If you look upon the travel industry as a branch of show business, you'll find it will all make sense,' he remarked.

At the time we were sitting beside each other in a private jet, being whisked down to the south of France to attend the annual convention of ABTA – the Association of British Travel Agents. The whisking was by courtesy of a major tour company, whose champagne was flowing freely, and I understood immediately what Mr Colegate was driving at.

Like the theatre or cinema, the travel trade sells the dream rather than the reality. A holiday can never be as perfect as the brochures promise, but we settle for the less than perfect – just as the publicity for the west end show or the latest blockbuster film is hype, but we still enjoy going to the theatre or the cinema. The characters who inhabit the UK tourist trade are, similarly, very much like larger-than-life showbiz types – or, rather, they were back then.

✈

After many months of following the herd, I thought I should break out on my own – find somewhere the others hadn't been to, go there and write about its potential as a holiday destination. I studied a large map of Europe for quite a while, ruling out the north and the east and deciding that what I needed was an unspoiled coastline with decent beaches, preferably facing south. The Mediterranean had very little to offer, but I saw that Portugal had just such a coast, sheltered from the north winds by the Monchique Mountains.

I contacted the London representative of the Portuguese National Tourist Office. We met and talked about this slice of his country which was apparently called the Algarve.

Nothing much was happening down there, he told me. As far as tourism to Portugal was concerned, people visited Lisbon and Porto. Those based in Lisbon went on side trips to Sintra or Estoril (in whose casino the character of James Bond was born). Those choosing Porto were likely to be interested in the Douro valley and the landscape of the north. Nobody went to the Algarve, he declared.

Naturally, I decided that is where I should go. He tried to dissuade me from this foolish course of action, but eventually agreed to contact his superiors in Lisbon and see what help they were willing to provide.

So it came to pass that, in the middle of October 1962, I flew to Lisbon for my first independent trip. There would be no other journalists to set my agenda, to keep me up late with their anecdotes and revelries or, most important, to share my discoveries.

I spent a pleasant night in a very decent Lisbon hotel before reporting, as planned, to the tourist office headquarters where I met a young man who was to be my driver and guide. All those years ago I did not possess a driving licence, you see. I could have travelled down to Faro by train, but the chaps in Lisbon didn't think the Algarve folk capable of looking after me as I needed to be looked after – what with me being an important English journalist.

In hindsight, I wish I had gone by train and trusted to luck, as my companion and guide proved to be a miserable lad who hated being out of Lisbon and thought the inhabitants of the deep south to be a bunch of useless peasants.

That afternoon we took the car ferry across the Tagus River – the bridge was several years away – and drove as far as Setúbal on the west coast for an overnight stay. Then we pressed on down that west coast, stopping overnight at Sines, before checking into a Pousada at Sagres, close to Cape St Vincent, the tip of Europe that the Portuguese call *el fim do mundo* – the end of the world.

Pousadas were a chain of state-owned hotels designed for people on the move. Like their Spanish counterparts, the Paradors, they provided accommodation for one or two nights, expecting their guests to be off about their business as soon as possible. This was perfect for the travelling salesmen who formed the bulk of their clients, but not much use to holidaymakers wanting to spend a week or more in the same place.

From the Pousada at Sagres we drove east along the coast, staying in a hotel near Monte Gordo called the Vasco da Gama, and in another Pousada at São Brás de Alportel. Along the entire stretch of coast, from Cape St Vincent to Vila Real de Santo António on the Spanish border, those were then pretty much the only hotels in the Algarve.

My miserable companion said there would, of course, be places where local people might stay, but these were of inferior quality and quite unsuitable for foreign visitors.

However, wherever we paused on our odyssey – and the trip was to take almost three weeks – I encountered wonderfully hospitable people. On learning I had come from London to check on the region's potential as a holiday destination they talked enthusiastically about their plans. Restaurateurs spoke of expanding their premises and opening new ones. The owners of those modest local hotels (which I insisted on visiting in spite of my companion's obvious disapproval) brought out blueprints for the extensions they were eager to build. The people of the Algarve, it seemed, were more than ready to welcome tourists.

So where were the visitors?

I concluded that the problem was a historic one. Situated down in the far south on the other side of the Monchique Mountains, the Algarve was a different country as far as the rest of Portugal was concerned. Its rulers had been designated kings of Portugal and the Algarve. Historically, it got little investment from the government in Lisbon and lagged behind in all areas of development. It was certainly a remote and undeveloped region then.

We spent days driving on narrow roads empty of traffic save for the occasional ox cart. To get to beaches we bumped down farm tracks, and found those beaches quite empty. On some, fishing boats had been hauled above the tide line and nets laid out to dry. That's what beaches were for, back then. Not for sitting on or sunbathing.

I remember arriving at one location to find two small girls playing on an upturned boat while their mother sat nearby beneath a parasol, engrossed in a book. When we got out of the car she waved and smiled. She was an Englishwoman whose husband was based in Lisbon. He would be joining them in a few days. Until then, the three of them had a wide and empty beach entirely to themselves. It was located at a tiny village called Carvoeiro – now an established holiday resort with several hundred holiday villas, more than three dozen hotels and over one hundred restaurants.

The Algarve then was a place where people came to their doors on hearing the unaccustomed sound of a car. Where they clearly thought the young Englishman must be mad to be taking photographs of empty beaches. There were no decent roads, and certainly no motorways. And it was to be a few years before Faro airport was built. Places that were to become large resorts were then just a handful of houses and the Algarve remained stubbornly unspoiled and virtually unchanged for a very long time – a destination my family and I came to love as, for several years, we took our holidays in villas and apartments all along that coast.

It couldn't stay that way, of course, especially after the opening of the airport, and I have a lot of regrets when I see what has happened to that gorgeous, empty, place.

But that's not the point of this particular essay.

The point is that, when I flew back to Heathrow, I was met by Ron Thorne, who ran a local cab company and regularly drove me between home and airports. I slung the case in his boot, climbed into the front passenger seat, and prepared for the journey home, and the usual small talk *en route*.

But Ron had a question for me.

'What do you think about the crisis?'

'What crisis?' I asked.

During my time in the Algarve, what was to become known as the Cuban Missile Crisis blew up. A stand-off between Nikita Khrushchev and Jack Kennedy, between the Soviet Union and the USA, brought the world to the brink of nuclear war. And I knew absolutely nothing about it. It was all over by the time I returned home.

I don't think many other journalists – or many other people, come to that – can make a similar claim.

The Burgundy Jacket
a 'faction'

Wilfred and Gloria Taylor did not seem to be in any way out of the ordinary when I met them on the first evening of a Mediterranean cruise with my family close on fifty years ago.

As custom dictates, the dress code that night was 'informal'; so I was unable to see them in their full finery until the following evening, when Black Tie was the rule for men, and what our young daughters called 'fairy frocks' for the ladies. For male passengers there was, back then, no alternative to the traditional black, the only variation being whether one's dinner jacket was single or double-breasted. So you may imagine the impact young Wilfred had when he appeared in a burgundy-coloured velvet jacket.

At least, I think it was burgundy.

I am not very good at colours, and thought it was closer to purple. One fellow passenger suggested plum – dark plum, of course. However, we finally settled on burgundy.

Wilfred's trousers were the acceptable black, as was his bow tie. His dress shirt was nothing to write home about. But his velvet jacket became a talking point as the evening – and the cruise – wore on. The debate about its exact colour was as nothing compared to the reaction of those older passengers for whom tradition meant much and anything other than black was striking at the very foundation of cruise etiquette.

Secretly, many of the ladies thought Wilfred Taylor was daring or even 'dashing' (and that's an adjective you don't hear much nowadays). But the inevitable male conclusion was that any chap who would wear such a garment must be a bit of a bounder.

'Bloody theatrical, if you ask me,' said Major Hawkins from his regular spot in the Midships Bar. And Mr Protheroe – who claimed to know a thing or two about the subject, having been 'in menswear' all his life – opined that it was the thin end of the wedge. (Mr Protheroe, who always introduced himself as 'an old cruise hand', was no stranger to a cliché.) Their wives sipped their Camparis and clucked agreement.

In blissful ignorance, young Wilfred continued to be his pleasant self to all and sundry (as, indeed, did the graceful Gloria). He wore his burgundy jacket on designated formal evenings and displayed it to fine advantage each time he whirled his wife around the dance floor after dinner.

'We bought it in Miami,' Gloria told me one evening towards the end of the trip, when curiosity got the better of me and I asked for the origin of Wilfred's splendid coat. 'In America, they don't have such rigid rules about the colour of a dinner jacket. Anyway, they call it a tuxedo, you know.'

I knew. And, having attended formal functions in the USA, I gave silent thanks that Wilfred had not been persuaded to invest in a more garish garment. Silver lamé, perhaps, or faux tartan. But I said nothing, for at that moment he joined us and whisked Gloria off for another trip around the dance floor.

As the years passed, I encountered the Taylors on a number of occasions – three times on ships of the Union Castle line going to South Africa, and four or five times on P&O cruises in the Mediterranean. During that time, the shipboard dress code became more relaxed. White jackets made their appearance – heaven knows what The Major and Mr Protheroe would have thought of that development – so Wilfred's burgundy garment did not stand out as much as it once had.

The passing years were reasonably kind to the Taylors, though they were not quite as nimble on the dance floor, and the jacket fitted a little more snugly as Wilfred's frame filled out.

I wondered why it had never been replaced, but Wilfred explained that Gloria liked him to wear it because, though undeniably shabby, it had become an essential part of their cruising wardrobe and their cruising ritual. I understood exactly what she meant, for the strongest of memories are founded on the slightest of things.

We exchanged cards at Christmas, and through the messages inside I knew that Wilfred was keeping reasonably fit, but was saddened to learn one year that Gloria was about to undergo major surgery.

Then there was silence. My inquiring letters went unanswered. Attempts to track down a telephone number failed. So I metaphorically shrugged my shoulders and went about my business – business that took me, in due course, to the Mediterranean and a lecturing stint on yet another cruise.

The day after joining the ship at Naples I walked around the Promenade Deck and, pausing by a rail to look down at the swimming pool area, saw Wilfred Taylor sitting in a deckchair.

Within minutes of joining him, I had the whole story.

Gloria had survived the surgery and they had gone on an extended visit to a son and daughter-in-law in South Africa – which explained the unanswered letters. The company of two lively grandchildren had, according to Wilfred, worked wonders. But there was a grim inevitability to her condition, and several months after returning home, Gloria had died. It had happened just six weeks previously. Wilfred had sunk into despair and distress, and his doctor had more or less ordered him to take a holiday.

That, then, was the story of the Taylors up to date. The story of a couple who loved cruising holidays and dancing together, and only made an impact on their fellow passengers all those years ago because of an unconventional dinner jacket worn by a young man whose new wife liked to see him in it, and who continued to admire it, even when it became ill-fitting and shabby.

✈

And that would have been that, had Wilfred not tried to grant Gloria's dying wish – to have her ashes scattered at sea from the Promenade Deck of a cruise ship. He had brought the urn with him, tucked away in his large suitcase, telling no-one of his intentions.

There is, of course, a well-established procedure for scattering ashes at sea. It happens more frequently than you might imagine, and a quiet word with the purser's staff sees a discreet ceremony arranged at which the captain or a senior officer says an appropriate prayer.

Unfortunately, Wilfred chose to perform the task himself and was discovered on the Promenade Deck late one evening in a state of considerable distress. Shaking the ashes from the urn, he had failed to allow for the wind which blew them back, covering him completely.

Supervised by the master-at-arms, two stewards carefully brushed ashes from Wilfred's burgundy jacket and his trousers, returning them to the urn with as much reverence as the situation allowed. Wisely, they ignored what was blowing about the deck.

The following afternoon, with the assistance of one of the guest lecturers who happened to be an Anglican priest, what remained of Gloria's ashes were cast on to the waves. The girls in the ship's shop had put the urn into a cardboard box, wrapping the whole in black crepe paper.

Also in the box was Wilfred's burgundy jacket.

'She loved that old coat,' he said, as we sat in the bar an hour or so later. 'I reckon what happened last night, with the wind and all, was her way of making sure she could take it with her. She'll have it cleaned and pressed and ready for me when it's my turn to go.'

I said nothing, as he downed a large Scotch and beckoned the barman for a refill.

However, I do believe that when he dresses for the formal evenings on that never ending celestial cruise, taking to the dance floor with his young bride, Wilfred's burgundy jacket will fit perfectly and look as smart as it did when I first saw it all those years ago.

Lights, Camera, Action!

Throughout the 1960s I travelled extensively around Eastern Europe. Though the Iron Curtain was firmly in place and the Cold War at its chilliest, those Eastern nations were trying to build up a tourism industry. They needed the hard currency it brought, and although under normal circumstances they reviled the hyenas of the wicked capitalist press, they had learned to live with the fact that they required help to promote tourism.

On one occasion, my travels took me to Bulgaria. It was a destination I approached with some caution, as fellow journalists had, on previous visits, tangled with the authorities, and come off worse. I was urged to do nothing which might upset my hosts who were, to put it mildly, suspicious of Western journalists – in fact, were paranoid about us. But to be fair, we were just as paranoid about them.

I flew into Sofia on a Balkan Airways flight, an experience which was more or less what I had anticipated. Nothing out of the ordinary happened until the plane landed and came to a standstill a little short of the airport building. Then an announcement was made to the effect that we should now hand over our passports to the flight attendants who would pass through the cabin and collect them.

Now this was a trifle unusual, and caused some concern among the holidaymaking passengers. It caused me more than some concern, as I was aware of my dodgy status in the eyes of my hosts.

As the passports were being collected, a set of stairs was wheeled up to the aircraft door. As soon as it was opened the passports were handed over and taken away by a uniformed official.

Then we waited. About ten minutes later two rifle-toting soldiers appeared at the front of the aircraft. One of them was holding a passport. An announcement was made asking that passenger Carter (pronounced 'Kair-tair') should make himself known to the cabin crew.

I raised my hand. One of the soldiers came down the plane towards me, indicating I should leave my seat and go with him. He was not smiling. Nor was his chum. Nor was I.

I left the plane, with every passenger watching my departure in stunned silence. Down the steps we went. The soldiers fell in on either side of me and marched me towards one of the airport buildings. We did not go inside, but swerved to the left and made our way to the back of the building – out of sight of the aircraft, I noted with some concern.

There, in a long straight line, were all the suitcases from the plane's hold. A man in a black suit, with a trilby hat fixed firmly on his head, indicated that I should identify my bag.

I did so, and stepped forward to pick it up. The man in the hat gestured me back and ordered one of the soldiers to bring the bag as we all walked into the building where a pair of Customs officers waited, grim-faced and unsmiling.

All sorts of thoughts were racing through my mind. Had they planted something in my suitcase that would enable them to lock me up for a couple of years or so? Was I, with or without suitcase, going to be taken for a ride to some secluded spot where my body would never be found? Was I perhaps going to be arrested in order to be exchanged for some Bulgarian spy who had been nabbed in London by our lot?

As I was trying to sort out my next move, one of the Customs chaps stepped forward. His right hand came out from behind his back. He was holding a large lump of chalk. He brought it down on to my case, scribbled a symbol upon it, then stepped back.

The man in the hat suddenly beamed with delight. As did the Customs chaps. And the soldiers.

'Welcome to Bulgaria, Mr Kair-tair,' he said.

I had just experienced the VIP welcome, Bulgarian style.

✈

So they allowed us into their countries, and we travelled around taking copious notes and attending meaningless meetings, which allowed the local bigwigs to scoff and quaff at state expense on the pretext of promoting their little part of the embryonic tourist industry.

We wrote many articles which helped popularise their new resorts, and after a while – when they realised we were, by and large, a fairly harmless bunch – the moles planted by the security services were replaced by genuine drivers and interpreters, and they stopped bugging the hotel rooms.

By then, we had all completed many fact-finding missions, returning home with our photographs and notes, our leaflets and brochures and impressions garnered from dozens of interviews and conversations, both formal and informal. And all sorts of other stuff, too.

Some of those impressions, and quite a lot of the 'other stuff', proved interesting to people back in London who were professionally required to be interested in such things, who had had informal chats with some of us before we departed on our jolly jaunts.

But none of that ever made it into print.

My favourite destination in those days was Yugoslavia, which was still held together by the force of Tito's personality, but already showing strong signs of an independent streak – a refusal to be dominated by the Soviet Union. I had a lot of fun in Yugoslavia – and a few adventures. One of those small adventures, which I wrote about all those years ago, began when I flew from Zagreb to Dubrovnik in a DC3. It had a clock on the bulkhead between the cockpit and the passenger cabin, and its seats were individual armchairs in uncut moquette. Then, Dubrovnik airport was nothing more than a large field with a single, grass-and-gravel landing strip and a windsock on a tall pole. Its buildings were a couple of wooden cabins under the trees.

As we walked towards those cabins, two men drove out in a flatbed truck, transferred the bags from the plane's hold to their vehicle, and drove back to dump them in a rough pile beside the cabins.

My suitcase was not in the rough pile. So I took myself off to a bench under a pine tree and sat down to await developments. What happened subsequently was more than a little surreal...

✈

The hefty lady in the bright national costume skipped up to me and thrust forward a large bunch of green grapes.

'No thank you,' I said.

She breathed deeply and the peasant blouse with its gay embroidery rose and fell with slow menace. Then the grapes were thrust forward once more.

'No thank you,' I repeated.

Another formidable lady approached, her long black skirt sweeping the grass. She had a basket of figs and a red hat, and a huge yellow tassel bouncing on her equally ample bosom.

'No thank you,' I said to the figs.

Then the first lady turned away and called the Yugoslav equivalent of: 'Hey, Charlie, come over here a minute, will you?'

Charlie was a small chap with scruffy overalls, a large moustache and wrinkles – lots of wrinkles.

'Hello, Charlie,' I said.

'Hello,' said Charlie. 'Are you English?'

I said I was. Just arrived on the plane from Zagreb. Going to Dubrovnik. During the flight, I realised I had mislaid my passport and now it appeared that my suitcase was missing, too.

'Don't worry about the passport,' said Charlie. 'It'll be in a pigeonhole behind the reception desk in your Zagreb hotel. Because they don't need it for internal flights, foreigners always forget to collect it when they leave.'

The moment he said that, I realised he was absolutely right.

'Do you have any more problems?' he asked.

'No,' I said. 'Except to tell these pleasant peasant ladies that I don't want to buy their grapes or their figs. Could you oblige?'

Charlie obliged.

'Actually,' he said, when they had gone, 'you don't need to worry about your suitcase, either. It'll be on the next flight.'

And it was, along with a lot of people who pounced on a pile of unclaimed cases from our plane.

As two flights left Zagreb for Dubrovnik within fifteen minutes of each other, nobody bothered to match up passengers and bags. As long as they all eventually ended up in that field near Dubrovnik, the authorities reasoned that there was no problem.

As I walked towards the bus with my suitcase, I looked for Charlie to say farewell, but he had wandered off and was sitting beneath a tree with two friends, a bottle of wine and the sort of conversation that needs at least six waving arms to give it momentum.

By this time the sun was sliding into the Adriatic and the light fading swiftly as we bounced over the rough coast road to Dubrovnik and my hotel, the Imperial.

'Do you make a habit of losing your passport?' the receptionist asked in a frosty tone when I presented myself at her counter.

'How did you know I had lost my passport?' I asked.

'The receptionist at your Zagreb hotel telephoned us to say you had left it behind. He is having it sent down on tomorrow morning's flight. It will be brought here. You have no need to worry about it.'

I should have realised that my itinerary had been issued in triplicate to every individual I was likely to encounter during my time in Yugoslavia. Of course the Zagreb hotel receptionist knew where I was going.

'I believe you are a journalist,' said the lady behind the counter. I much admired the 'I believe' part. Of course she knew I was a journalist. It would be on those triplicated documents – along with my shoe size, marital status and alcohol capacity.

I confirmed that I was, indeed, a journalist, and I was gathering material for travel articles, though this was not strictly true. I was actually on the run from Italian film companies.

Yugoslavia was waist-deep in Italian film companies making low-budget spectaculars wherever they could. The hotel in Zagreb had housed two of them, the *Gladiatrici* crew and another mob making a film about Genghis Khan – at least, I think it was about Genghis Khan. At the time he was a popular subject for the sort of films that had little plot but a lot of men with serious beards, strutting around in high boots brandishing scimitars. These films also featured much fighting and, at every opportunity, comely maidens dressed in diaphanous robes dancing in what the director thought was a sinuously tempting fashion. All I know for sure about the film makers in my Zagreb hotel is that they didn't go to bed until around 3 a.m. and got up at seven to check their equipment, have hysteria outside my bedroom door, and depart for their location in very old buses.

But I could not tell the young lady all this, so I said I was gathering material for travel articles.

'There is an Italian film company in Dubrovnik,' she said. 'They are making a film called *The Green Sword of Genghis Khan*, with very many local people employed as extras. It is good for our economy.'

I met them next day as I explored the streets. They were, for the most part, young Yugoslav lads in false beards and cardboard armour, giggling furiously and scampering around the ramparts, brandishing their halberds. I peeped over the wall on the seaward side and saw a ship sailing to and fro with another small boat behind it, bearing a camera crew. Then one of the Yugoslavs clonked me with his halberd and indicated that I should keep out of the shot.

If that ancient epic ever surfaces on a late-night movie channel, do watch it carefully, because the fellow who peeps over the rampart and gets clonked by a halberd is me.

About half an hour later I found myself at the top of what my guidebook told me was one of the city's ancient towers. But when I compared it with the picture, I realised some twenty extra feet had sprouted from somewhere. It looked a pretty solid sort of tower, not the sort that grows overnight; it must have been many centuries old.

But it was made of canvas.

'Fancy going up?' asked a voice. It was Charlie – in armour.

'No thanks,' I said.

Charlie told me that the Italian company had built this tower at great expense, and now wanted someone to leap from it into the sea. For money.

When Charlie told me how much, I was half way up the steps, tearing my shirt off for the plunge, but he pointed out the snag. Apparently, in order to survive one would have to leap outwards about fifteen feet before starting to fall, and this was a very tricky manoeuvre. Professional jumpers-off-high-places had flocked to Dubrovnik like migrating swallows when their grapevine had spread the news of the loot to be had. But they had all gone home fairly swiftly on seeing the problem. One Spaniard hadn't even bothered to get out of his taxi.

The passport turned up in my hotel pigeonhole that evening. A different reception lady examined it closely – especially all the stamps from all the countries I had visited. I was clearly the sort of chap to be viewed with great suspicion.

'Are you going to report on the film?' she asked. I said I was not, but she went on as if I had not spoken. 'It is an Italian company, you know. It's called *The Red Sword of Genghis Khan*.'

'Don't you mean '*Green*'?' I asked.

'No,' she said. 'My cousin is playing a part in it. He should know.'

I was very sorry to leave Dubrovnik, feeling that another week there would have seen me starring in *The Purple Dagger of Henry VIII*, or at least getting a substantial role in someone else's production of *Genghis Khan's Last Stand*. But I had to go to sample the delights of Split, and the island of Hvar.

A few days later, in the middle of thinking how splendid Hvar was, I saw a pre-war London Transport Green Line bus come slowly into view and roll to a neat standstill a yard or so away from the café at one of whose pavement tables I was sitting.

'Is there an Italian film company on Hvar, making *The Green Bus of St Trinian's*?' I asked my hostess at dinner that evening. She said there was not, but the bus was certainly real and British visitors got the giggles whenever they saw it. Needless to say, nobody had any idea how it got there.

'It is strange you should mention Italian film companies,' she said. 'There is one in Dubrovnik at the moment, filming an epic about Charlemagne. It is employing lots of Yugoslav extras, which is good for the economy.'

'Is there a Yugoslav film industry?' I asked, choosing not to get into an argument about Genghis Khan or Charlemagne.

She assured me that there was. Indeed, it was flourishing, though the shortage of extras would have to be tackled very soon, as Yugoslavia was running out of young men who could cope with false beards and cardboard armour. I suggested this could be done by shipping out surplus members of British amateur operatic and dramatic societies, who couldn't be fitted into *Oklahoma* or *The Student Prince*. She did not take this seriously, which is a pity, as it could have proved a profitable venture all round.

It was at the Motel Paklenica near Stari Grad that the final blow fell. I was in a restaurant beside a country road, eating cubes of meat on skewers which I had learned by then not to call kebabs, when I noticed some men building frameworks beside the road.

'They're constructing a film set, aren't they?' I asked.

My companion sipped his Grk and nodded.

'An outdoor epic?'

He nodded again.

'An Italian company making a film about Genghis Khan's Silver Sword, Allah's Green Dagger, Charlemagne's Mighty Battleaxe, or the Mysterious East in general?'

He shook his head, put down his glass of wine and plied a toothpick with some vigour before replying.

'Actually, no. It's a Spanish company, over here to make a Western, *The Black Gun of Billy the Kid*. And they will employ lots of Yugoslav extras, which is good for the economy.'

✈

I must add a couple of footnotes to this story. The first is that the film *Gladiatrici*, whose crew I encountered at the start of my trip, was to become an example of the worst kind of sword-and-sandals epic. Its title translates as 'Women Gladiators', but it was also known as 'Thor and the Amazon Women'. On its release in 1963 it was generally judged to be, in the words of one critic, 'about as bad as they come'. Probably for this reason, scenes from it may be viewed on the internet to this day.

The second footnote is that a few months after that trip, I was back in Yugoslavia, first making my way from Sarajevo to Dubrovnik by bus, then, after enjoying a couple of days at that city's arts festival, going a little way south along the coast to Sveti Stefan. This tiny fishing village, snug within its high medieval walls, had been transformed into a luxury hotel, with its inhabitants happily relocated to modern homes a short distance away. The old cottages were now suites, and the entire place was a gem, of which the Yugoslavs were understandably proud. I had met the hotel's manager in London a few weeks previously and, hearing I would be in the neighbourhood, he had insisted I stay at Sveti Stefan for a night or so. And so it came to pass.

A message awaited my arrival. The manager regretted that we could not dine *à deux*, as planned, as he had unexpectedly to entertain two VIPs. This was not an unusual situation: as I mentioned, local bigwigs and assorted Party officials took every opportunity to gatecrash any kind of event that afforded them free food or wine.

They were a monstrous nuisance, the men being boors and the wives, for the most part, unattractive, overweight women with bleached blonde hair, fur coats, and absolutely no English. I braced myself for just such company as I made for the bar where I had been told my host would be waiting. He was.

Beside him was a short, bald man who, I decided, was probably the manager of a local tractor factory, in good standing with the Party. Sitting on a bar stool, with her back to me, was his wife, wearing the obligatory fur, but with black, not bleached blonde, hair. To my delight, the hotel manager announced my arrival to them in English. At least conversation would be possible. As I drew close, the fur-clad lady swung round to greet me.

She was Sophia Loren. The little bald chap was Carlo Ponti.

What followed was a very memorable encounter. Towards its end, when a fair amount of wine had been consumed, I asked Carlo Ponti why he and his good lady were travelling in style around Yugoslavia as guests of the government.

'I am here to find suitable locations for the many films I intend to make in Yugoslavia,' he replied, but the twinkle in his eyes told me that wasn't quite true.

A little while, and a lot more wine, later, he admitted that he and his wife were simply having a splendid, all expenses paid, holiday, and he had no plans to film anything in Yugoslavia.

As far as I know, he never did.

My Colleagues
and Other Animals

A nybody who regularly travels abroad with colleagues will tell you that nearly every trip generates a running joke.

Something happens at the outset that sets off a train of thought and creates amusement. At the time, the joke is absolutely hilarious, building to a climax more or less as you are preparing for the journey home. However, the passing of time causes it to lose its lustre and it is quite impossible to explain the joke to anyone who wasn't there. If you have been in such a situation you will know exactly what I mean.

An example of this concerns the opening ceremonies for the Royal Teheran Hilton hotel, back when the Shah was still on the Peacock Throne and Iran was still called Persia. The hotel, incidentally, is now the Parsian Esteghlal International, so there. Hilton was then a major international chain, much favoured by business types who wanted to travel the globe but stay, essentially, in middle America. Wherever they went, Hilton would provide a familiar standard of comfort, service, food and drink. The staff would speak English, know how to mix a martini and produce a decent steak dinner. The king-sized bed would be exactly the same wherever in the world it happened to be, as would the trouser press and the facilities in the en-suite bathroom.

Along with a bunch of journalists and celebrities from all over the globe, I was invited to the grand opening of their Teheran property.

Everything was complimentary from the moment you checked in for your flight to the Persian capital to the moment you landed back home. You could even take as a souvenir the smart brass carriage clock on your bedside table, along with your bulging goodie bag of brochures, pens and notebooks, cosmetics and so forth. Indeed, I have that little brass carriage clock on a bedside table to this very day.

All would have gone off splendidly, had not Hilton's great rivals, the Sheraton chain, chosen that week to announce plans to build a hotel near the Mount of Olives in Jerusalem.

The Hilton press officers believed – probably correctly – that Sheraton had done this deliberately in order to steal their publicity. They fulminated mightily in the bars and lounges of the Royal Teheran Hilton, threatening revenge.

It was at this moment that I came up with a solution, suggesting that Hilton could retaliate by building a hotel of their own in Bethlehem, calling it the Jesus Christ Hilton. Unfortunately I made this suggestion out loud in the presence of press officers and fellow travel writers. The joke took off.

As days went by, details of this mythical hotel were supplied by the assorted press corps. The American journalists took a while to catch on, but when they did their contributions were gratefully accepted.

The Jesus Christ Hilton would have a Loaves and Fishes Grill and a King of Kings-sized swimming pool ('for guests who wished to take a stroll after dinner'). It would also provide a King Herod baby-minding service, a late night Last Supper room, the Judas Iscariot Grill with meals at a fixed price of thirty pieces of silver. Other details revolved, naturally, around turning water into wine and feeding five thousand. As I recall, the Joseph and Mary 'manger-style' honeymoon suite was particularly well received.

It was all in very bad taste, but nobody took offence – at least, nobody among the press corps, whose members included those of Christian and Jewish persuasion and, for all I know, Muslims, Hindus, Mormons, Seventh Day Adventists, Flat-Earthers and anybody else you care to name. However, our hosts suffered a major sense of humour failure, with the result that I was put on a blacklist, receiving no invitations from Hilton for a considerable time. They brought me in from the wilderness when they decided to build a hotel in Paris – indeed they consulted me about the media invitation list even. But what happened unexpectedly on that occasion will have to be told some other time...

Oh, gosh, I'm running off at a tangent again. Sorry. I must keep my thoughts on the subject of how travelling with colleagues can make a tremendous difference to a trip – whether it's because they join in the fun and contribute to the running joke, or whether they simply, by their presence, transform what would otherwise be a mundane or routine experience.

That's how things turned out on a trip to Corfu. A trip that didn't hold out much promise, to be frank. The organisers had decided to mix travel writers with travel agents. This rarely works, for we have different priorities and agendas, and unite only in the bar or the restaurant – mainly to argue. On our second evening we gathered in one of Corfu town's smartest hotels for a folklore performance. I have firm ideas about folklore performances, as you will realise as you travel through these pages; suffice it to say that I have attended more than my fair share. This particular event consisted, in the main, of Greek girls prancing around, swishing their multi-layered petticoats and waving large handkerchiefs whilst moustachioed Greek chaps – most of whom were named Spiro for religious reasons – tried to whisk them off their feet. As the girls were fairly hefty and the chaps were not, the whisking was largely unsuccessful.

What set this performance apart, however, was a lady named Madame Aspioti (MBE) who appeared on the stage from time to time to tell us what was going to happen next. She was quite small, dressed in a green tweed suit, with brown stockings and sensible brown shoes. She looked not unlike a field mouse with gangrene.

Educated at Cheltenham Ladies College, she said things like: 'The costumes are of Byzantoiyn desoiyn' and went into great detail concerning the background and history of each dance or song that was to follow. She introduced one song by explaining that the singer was supposed to be a shepherd tending his flock on the hillside above the village. The lyric, she explained, translated as:

'My love has eyes for another, but I shall not despair for I smell octopus and rice.'

I looked at the chap sitting to my left, who happened to be the president of the Association of British Travel Agents, and to the chap on my right, the travel editor of *The Daily Express*. Both confirmed that my ears had not deceived me. So I wrote it all down in my notebook as the Corfiot gent – named Spiro, of course – belted out his lament.

After the performance, I made a beeline for Madame Aspioti (MBE) as she sat in the lounge. Hot on my heels were the aforementioned travel editor, David Ash, and Arthur Eperon, who'd been travel editor of the old *Daily Herald* as well as *The Sun*, and was to go on to write for ITV's *Wish You Were Here…?* as well as produce a copious number of books. We all questioned Madame Aspioti (MBE) about the shepherd's song.

Madame Aspioti (MBE)'s explanation was that octopus and rice was the traditional dish eaten at the feast to celebrate a betrothal. The shepherd knew that it was being prepared for the betrothal of him and his beloved.

'But according to this damned song he knows that she has eyes for another,' protested David.

'And despite that, he's going through with it,' I added. 'Have we got this right?'

Madame Aspioti (MBE) nodded.

'I have to tell you, madam,' declared Arthur grimly, 'that this is no basis for a happy marriage. I have some experience of the world, and I can assure you – and that bloody shepherd – that nothing good will come of this.'

The following day we hired a car, having decided that time away from our group, not to mention our minders, might produce some useful copy. Not that we disliked our group, mind you. They were, without exception, jolly souls whose company was lively. Unfortunately, that is exactly the kind of situation in which little real work can be done and, despite what everyone thinks to the contrary, work has to be done during such jaunts.

We headed for the northeast corner of the island, then – in the mid 1960s – controlled by the military and out of bounds because of its proximity to Albania, a country whose rulers were gripped by paranoia and whose border guards had an unfortunate tendency to shoot first without even bothering to ask subsequent questions. David and I shared the driving while Arthur sat contentedly in the back seat, helping with the navigation, until he dozed off after lunch.

We headed further into the forbidden zone until we came to a road block and a couple of young soldiers with rifles. They were not pleased to see us, and shouted a lot. This was perfectly understandable and we tried to convince them we were stupid English tourists who had got lost. They spoke no English; we spoke no Greek. It was *impasse* until a young lieutenant showed up. His English was excellent, and he was responding nicely to our abject apologies when Arthur woke.

Taking in the situation at a glance, he leaned forward and said, a little too loudly: 'Best make out we're just ordinary tourists. For goodness sake don't let on we're JOURNALISTS.'

It took an awfully long time to get the subsequent situation sorted out. We were hauled off to a sort of Portakabin and shouted at until a major arrived, who merely escalated the seriousness of the shouting. There were telephone calls and long awkward silences, until one of the original young soldiers appeared with tin mugs of coffee. This clearly marked an improvement in Anglo-Greek relations and by the time we drove away there were some thin and hesitant smiles from all sides. All's well that ends moderately well, I suppose.

We spent a few more days racing around Corfu with the travel agents and local tourism officials, inspecting too many hotels and meeting too many coach operators, restaurant owners, and the like, before deciding it was time to break away again. We hired another car and headed south, planning to go as far as possible in a day. The direction was not chosen randomly. For one thing, it would take us far away from the northeast corner and potential military confrontation. It could also provide material for some travel articles. Back then, the region beyond Messonghi was undeveloped. The road was virtually non-existent, our hire car temperamental and the journey something of an adventure: ideal conditions for the manufacture of a decent travel piece.

Around midday we stopped for coffee and to stretch our legs, then pressed on to a spot on the coast, far below Perivoli. To be frank, we were beginning to think the decision to head south had been a bad one. There had been nothing of interest along the route, though the little beaches were attractive, or would be if they hadn't been blighted by litter. The coast road was hard to follow and had been neglected, though clearly it was sufficient for whoever was fly-tipping rubbish on those beaches. This seemed to be a part of the island for which nobody was taking responsibility. And yet, I couldn't shake off the thought that it had potential. In a scrubby, desolate landscape on the edge of a small beach was a taverna. No other building was in sight, so for better or worse, this was where we would eat before heading back.

As we approached, a man appeared in the doorway at the back of the building, shading his eyes from the sun and calling out to us. It was not a greeting, but a question, to judge from the inflexion of his voice. We drew close enough for him to realise we were not the people he was expecting. As soon as he knew we were English he switched to our language. A former merchant seaman, he had learned the *lingua franca* of the professional traveller. On retirement, he had sunk his savings in the taverna, hoping for success and prosperity when the tourist tide flowed south, as it inevitably should (and, indeed, inevitably did).

A few minutes after our arrival another car pulled up and two men and a woman emerged. One man was a doctor, the woman a midwife, and the other chap had, about an hour previously, been sent by our host to fetch them. In a room above the restaurant, the owner's young wife was about to produce their first child. He was, he acknowledged, a little old to be a new father, but hoped he would be up to the task.

We spent the next few hours helping him get through the experience. This help consisted mainly of drinking a lot of rough red wine and encouraging him to do the same. He had closed the restaurant (customers were pretty thin on the ground anyway), and in any case had no inclination to cook. Arthur, who was pretty handy in the saucepan department, headed into the kitchen and produced a very good meal, given the circumstances.

At around 9 p.m. we all trooped upstairs to the bedroom and raised our glasses in a heartfelt toast to this splendid man, his pretty, young, and thoroughly exhausted, wife and their brand-new daughter.

Then we drove north.

Very, very carefully.

The Villa

When our children were young, we used villas as our holiday accommodation. It was the most sensible option, enabling us to eat when we wished, and not when a hotel's timetable said we could. Children want things to be as much like home as possible, and at home you don't have to wait for lunch when you're hungry. There were lots of other advantages, too, of course, but that was the main one.

The travel trade calls such holidays 'self-catering' which is a marketing own goal, conjuring up visions of someone (guess who?) spending lots of time in the kitchen while husband and offspring relax by the pool.

We chose the 'no-catering' option. At the earliest opportunity we'd buy orange juice and coffee and breakfast cereals from the nearest supermarket, so we could breakfast at leisure in our villa. Other meals were taken in local restaurants. Or we'd pig out on pizzas as we sunbathed on our veranda with no thought for timetables.

I must boast that our three children were perfectly behaved when we took them to restaurants – so much so that fellow diners would sometimes come to our table to tell us how they admired our kids. At the time we didn't think their behaviour out of the ordinary, but over the years I have learned that it was. The secret, if there was one, was that we introduced them to restaurants at an early age and treated them like grown-ups, which they desired and appreciated. This even extended to allowing them to drink a glass of wine – extremely diluted, of course. The result was that, as far as they were concerned, eating in restaurants was no big deal, so there was no need to make a fuss about it – and, as far as children are concerned, 'making a fuss' means showing off and misbehaving. Which ours never did.

We enjoyed such holidays in Portugal and Spain, and share wonderful memories of them all – including the time when Susan and Sarah conspired with their mother to smuggle a baby hare on to the flight home from Faro. Portugal, in particular, was a great destination, back when it was still Europe's best-kept secret. Yet, it is our experience of a villa on the island of Minorca that I particularly remember.

We'd booked it through one of the UK-based firms that sell the whole deal as a package – flights and maid service included, along with a welcome pack of groceries to get you started and a hire car if you so desired. We duly arrived at Minorca airport late one summer afternoon to be greeted by a young lady with a clipboard, who directed us to a waiting coach.

The coach gradually filled up with fellow travellers, mostly youngish parents with small children, like us. Then we set off from the airport and, after a while, began to drop people off close to the villas they had chosen.

We were among the last passengers to be so deposited. As we took the suitcases from the compartment in the coach, Miss Clipboard said the company's local representative was unfortunately unable to meet us, as planned, but that the key to the villa could be collected from the owner of a bar just a few paces away.

We were not happy about this, as we had hoped the local rep would see us safely to our door. However, I collected the key from the bar owner who gave me directions to the villa. This involved a lot of waving and smiling on his part, and much nodding and smiling on mine.

Key and suitcases in hand, we trudged along the lane as darkness fell. There were, of course, no street lights, but the chap in the bar had lent me a torch, so we were able to avoid the worst of the potholes.

We finally reached the villa. The key wouldn't open the front door.

Leaving wife, children and luggage behind, I scouted round the back of the property. The key wouldn't open the back door, either.

'That idiot in the bar must have given me the wrong key,' I said, when I returned to my waiting wife and kids, for I had noticed that he had a board there with several keys and empty hooks on it. But I was in no mood to go trailing back to the bar for the correct key. It was late, we were all tired and hot and scruffy from the journey. So I decided to break in.

I returned to the rear of the property, found a suitable window, broke it, and clambered in. I stumbled through the pitch black villa to the front door, opening it and admitting my family.

It didn't take long to find the fuse box and put the lights on. But I was not very happy with our situation. None of the beds were made, so we had to get pillows and sheets from a cupboard and make them ourselves. The rep from the villa renting company was going to get it in the neck when we met the following morning, that was for sure.

To make matters worse the promised welcome pack of groceries was not in the kitchen, even though we had paid for it as part of the deal. The refrigerator was empty, too.

We were, at least, able to sluice down the children and get them to bed, with the last of the snacks and sweets we had packed for the journey. Then we all spent a fitful night.

Came the dawn – or rather, a little while after the dawn – and we all trooped back down to the bar to get some breakfast and an explanation from the rep. We were, as you may imagine, in a pretty sour mood and ready to rip her apart.

Julie arrived as we were finishing our orange juices and croissants and coffees. She looked drained and anxious.

Before I could say anything, she launched into an explanation for her absence the previous evening. Her small daughter had developed a painful earache and, fearing it could be something serious, she and her husband had whipped her into the local hospital's A&E department.

But, she explained, she had taken great care to ring the bar owner and tell him which property we were renting.

Then I gave her our side of the story. She listened in stunned silence.

'I am positive Juan would have given you the correct key,' she said. 'And I know for a fact that the beds were all made and the welcome pack was left on the kitchen table, because I left it there myself and, when I did so, I checked all the bedrooms.'

This mystery needed solving, so we piled into her car and bounced off along the potholed lane.

After a few moments we reached the villa in which we had spent the night.

However, it was not the villa we had rented.

That villa was on the other side of the track, more or less opposite to ours. Julie knew that the one we had broken into belonged to a German family, who kept it for their own use when they came to Minorca every summer. She also happened to know that they would be arriving the following afternoon.

So we had the rest of the day to unmake those beds, clean the bathroom, remove all traces of our overnight occupation. And get the broken window replaced.

With the help of Julie, the owner of the bar, and the girl who was to provide our 'maid service' – who all thought it was the funniest thing that had happened in those parts for many a long year – we managed it.

However, we kept a low profile when our German neighbours appeared. He was a very hefty, sour-faced bloke, and struck me as being the sort of fellow who would not regard my error as a laughing matter.

Blazing Poodles

When I was a callow newcomer to the travel writing game (well, reasonably callow), I accepted every invitation that came my way, fearing that they might dry up, leaving me to my own devices. I thought my own devices would not be enough to sustain me in the style of life to which I was becoming accustomed, which is – in part – why I found myself on Mainland in January 1967.

Mainland, I must explain, is the name of the largest of the Shetland Isles, and it is so called in order to confuse everybody. However, when a visitor points out, reasonably, that Scotland is the proper mainland, a local will, just as reasonably, point out that Scotland itself is part of an island.

It is at this stage of the conversation that drink is taken in order to clear the head.

The journey there was in its own way rather strange, and should have alerted me to what was ahead. We gathered early one afternoon in the bar of a London hotel – we being half a dozen travel hacks and a team of officials from what was then called the British Travel Association – for a little light refreshment before setting out. We were to fly from Gatwick Airport, so I had assumed the waiting minibus would whisk us and our luggage to the terminal without delay.

In this I was wrong. For reasons best known to themselves, the officials of the British Travel Association had decreed we would overnight in Kent and fly off the following morning. Our destination was the village of Penshurst – specifically a 15th-century inn called The Spotted Dog. We ate and drank at that ancient hostelry, slept well and left for Gatwick early the following morning.

The journey took just about all day, which is why we hadn't been able to start the previous evening. We first flew to Edinburgh. Then to somewhere else near Aberdeen. The airport near Aberdeen had obviously been an RAF field, with a lot of camouflage paint and Nissen huts about, and a distinct lack of amenities. From there we headed out over the grim North Sea to the Shetlands. Our purpose: to attend the Up Helly Aa festival. The journey had been a strange one. The Shetlands were even stranger...

✈

'Why aren't those crows flying?' I asked the driver, but he accelerated to a frisky fifteen miles an hour, muttering something about 'bliddy sooth-moother'.

There were these crows, you see. Trudging along the roadside from the airport towards Lerwick, they were, and the sight of them made me realise that Shetland was going to be different.

We roared up towards Scalloway with sheep and ponies watching our progress through the mist, and occasional cyclists passing us, jeering as they did so. I had come to Shetland for an ancient Viking festival, and my thoughts were in turmoil by the time we arrived at the harbour. I thanked my driver, but he growled off into the gloom and I never saw him again. I believe he was spirited away by Krash, the pagan god of taxi drivers.

The Shetlands have strange names about them, like Unst and Fetlar, Whalsay and Papa Stour and they are, of course, Norse. Even more so are they on the last Tuesday in January which marks the winter solstice and is the day of the festival. Then, from Saxa Vord and

Gloup, from Northmavine, Vidlin and Sandness, the sturdy islanders trudge into Lerwick.

'Up Helly Aa' they call it, and they practise this call throughout the year on the nearby island of Yell – sacred to Ton-sil, pagan goddess of shouting.

'Why do all the crows walk on this island?' I asked Colin, who deftly relieved me of my fears and my luggage and conjured up a welcoming glass from the hotel bar.

'You will find out soon enough,' he said, smiling grimly.

I looked out of the window and saw three more crows plodding through the downpour. So we drank a toast to Drench, pagan goddess of rain. It rained upon the crows and they scampered for cover, cursing crow curses all the while.

The origins of the Up Helly Aa festival are lost in the mists of antiquity which swirl – looking suspiciously like mists of rain – around Shetland most of the time. It could be a thanksgiving for the end of winter and the coming of spring. It could be something to do with Lent. It could be basically sexual in character. It could be good for the tourist trade.

Which is why we were there.

Each year a festival committee of sixteen elect one of their number to be Guizer Jarl – the head bloke, or 'Chief Geezer', as one of my companions suggested. It is the Jarl who rides triumphant in the Viking galley as a squad of men pull it through the Lerwick streets and others march and counter-march, bearing flaming torches and clad in strange costumes.

The men from the British Travel Association thought it would be a good thing if Shetland held a similar kind of Viking festival in summer to attract tourists.

'What do you think?' I asked the Jarl, imposing in his Viking armour and bearing his Viking sword. He voiced his disapproval vehemently. However, I had another, much more important question.

'Why are all the crows walking?'

The Jarl smiled a thin smile and slowly fingered his beard. 'You will soon find out,' he said.

We drank toasts to Kramp, the pagan god of writers. Then the Jarl strode, clanking, into the night, aiming a kick at a passing crow as he went. The time had come for Up Helly Aa.

Outside, the torches were lit and bands began to play as the great fire march began. The mast of the galley appeared between chimney pots and then, quite suddenly, the reason for the walking crows was revealed.

Each noble Viking had on his head a noble Viking helmet – decorated with feathers fixed on to look like wings.

'Crow's wings,' gasped my friend Harry. 'Oh, the pagan devilry of it all.'

We turned our eyes from the terrible sight, thanking the pagan gods that, at least, the ravens had been spared. But worse was to come, for the assorted torch-bearing squads had dressed themselves in strange garments.

Alongside the Vikings were men dressed as poodles, men dressed as apes, men dressed as Fyfe Robertson and even – horror of all horrors! – spotted Diddy-men. All bore flaming torches.

'Pyromaniacs,' screamed Harry, but his scream was snatched by the wind and borne away by Kole, pagan god of fire.

Then, carrying more torches, came men dressed as women.

'Transvestite pyromaniacs,' I yelled. The situation was by now hopeless. There was but one thing to be done. We did it. We abandoned ourselves to the pagan revelries. We knew there would be Viking songs and Viking dances under the timbered roof of the town hall and felt we had no choice but to embrace whatever fate had in store. Dances and songs there were. We naturally expected wild, abandoned behaviour with drinking songs and flagons of ale. To end up in a community centre watching the sensuous movements of the Boston Two Step and sinuous rhythms of the St Bernard Waltz – danced by poodles – was a bit of a dampener. Lerwick may be the only part of the United Kingdom where young men and women know all the words of the sentimental ballad 'Ramona'.

The night wore on. Dedicated as it was to Insomnia, pagan goddess of travel journalists, we could not leave, and the grey dawn found me walking the damp streets of Lerwick with a man who had invented a decimal alphabet.

We stood, silently, on the edge of the quay and watched the still waters bobbing with fishing boats and empty whisky bottles. To each boat was attached an anchor. To each bottle, a man.

'There has been a ritual sacrifice here,' said my friend. 'To Malt, the pagan god of hangovers.'

And so we said farewell to Lerwick. Above our heads the screaming seagulls wheeled and swooped. Around our feet the sad crows scampered. Up Helly Aa had come and gone.

'I'm glad I'm not a Viking', said Harry.

'I'm glad I'm not a crow,' I replied.

✈

The article I wrote as a result of this trip was syndicated to the group of regional newspapers for which I worked. When it appeared in the Aberdeen *Evening Express*, it brought a certain amount of Celtic wrath down upon my head. I managed to survive it.

Years later, I visited a very different Shetland – by then enjoying the wealth that oil had brought. I discovered then that though winter fire festivals are of ancient origin, Up Helly Aa in its present form dates, in fact, only from the 1880s. The enthusiastic London-based chaps from the British Travel Association had, however, overlooked a basic problem when they tried to persuade the Shetlanders to hold some sort of summer fire festival.

You need darkness to appreciate the true nature of a fire festival. In summer, in the Shetlands, it doesn't get dark.

The Joker
a 'faction'

I am happiest when cruising on small ships, those with well under 500 passengers. That is what I consider a manageable number, though the disadvantage is that it is difficult to avoid people whose company you'd prefer to do without. Such folk are few and far between in my perhaps fortunate experience – but when you do come across them, they are a terrible pain in the neck.

Which brings me to Danny Dunston, a fellow passenger on *Ethos*, an elderly vessel with a chequered history and a string of aliases, ending her days ploughing around the eastern Mediterranean under the Greek flag.

Along with a director and film crew, I had boarded *Ethos* at Piraeus to film a story for our television travel show, the angle being to report how British passengers got on with those of other nationalities. For, unlike most ships aimed at the UK market, *Ethos* was a multinational vessel. The Brits on board were in a minority, with German, French, Italian and Greek passengers taking the bulk of the berths. On this particular sailing there happened to be a handful of Canadians and Americans, who became 'honorary Brits' for the duration of the voyage, bound as we were by a common language – well, almost.

We discovered early on that it was fun to mingle, even if we couldn't always understand what people were saying; though, to their credit, nearly everyone understood and spoke enough English to get by. To our shame, the British contingent didn't appear to have any linguistic skills whatsoever.

Short, fat Danny Dunston was a Yorkshireman, travelling alone and making no attempt to integrate. Danny had little regard for 'foreigners' and spent most of his time being rude about them. This rudeness came in the form of jokes – or what he thought were jokes, though few of us found them amusing.

'Hey, Johnny,' he would yell, bearing down on me in the Forward Lounge, or on the Sun Deck. 'Here, have you heard this one?' Then came the joke, which revolved around the stupidity of other nationalities and relied on the worst kind of stereotyping.

Mercifully, time has driven most of them from my memory, and in any case they would not bear repeating. All this happened a good many years ago when Political Correctness had not been invented, and even mainstream comedians had a few racial gags that were acceptable to audiences of the time. Think Bernard Manning, and you've got the picture. But Danny Dunston was not a mainstream comedian. He was not any kind of comedian. However, like many little, chubby blokes he'd cast himself in the role of jester and there was no stopping him. And no avoiding him.

'Somebody ought to kill that awful man,' declared Kathy, striding into the bar one evening. Kathy was a splendid lady (still is, as it happens), a very efficient production assistant and a great travelling companion. She got on with most people, but not with Danny Dunston.

I bought her a drink as she described how he had waylaid her a few minutes earlier and insisted on telling yet another of his unfunny stories.

'Was it the one about the Greek waiter and the honeymoon couple?' asked Roy, the cameraman. 'That is really gross.'

'Or the German, the Frenchman and the Italian wrecked on the desert island?' enquired Robin, our sound recordist. 'Very vulgar and not at all funny.'

'That sentence describes the little squirt perfectly,' retorted Kathy. 'Oh, God, how I need another drink.'

As the trip was nearing its end, and just when we thought the 'little squirt' situation couldn't get much worse, the ship's daily bulletin announced there would be a passenger talent show in the Forward Lounge two evenings hence. Danny Dunston declared he was going to take part and the entire English-speaking contingent – including the Yanks and the Canadians – went into a state of shock.

Surely he couldn't be that thick-skinned? Surely he would have more sense than to deliver those awful jokes to the Germans and the Greeks, the French and the Italians, who knew enough English to understand and be more than merely offended at them?

Hard though we tried, we couldn't come up with a plan to stop him participating. Kathy rejected out of hand a suggestion that she might keep him occupied on the evening in question – not that we seriously considered such a sacrifice, you understand, but by then we were clutching at straws.

The evening of the talent show arrived. We fortified ourselves at the bar, waited until the lounge was full, then slipped into a rear corner by the doors – handy for a quick exit. Tom, our director, reckoned there would certainly be a riot and wondered whether we ought to film it. Camera and Sound said something along the lines of 'over our dead bodies' so we left the gear in the cabins.

The show began.

A Frenchman played a guitar fairly well. A German lady recited a long poem which went down well with the Germans, but was lost on the rest of us. Four Italian youngsters mimed to a tape of ABBA, which I thought was internationalism gone mad.

Then came the moment we were dreading.

The curtains parted. The little fat man toddled into the spotlight, looked towards the side of the stage, and gave a slight nod.

A piano began to play. And Danny Dunston began to sing.

From the first words of 'Some Enchanted Evening', it was obvious that this was no ordinary amateur's voice, but a fine, trained baritone, a voice that made your skin tingle. I glanced at Kathy who was staring, open-mouthed, at the man in the spotlight. And saw her eyes fill with tears as the lyrics told their tale.

The last line ended, there was a long moment's silence then the audience erupted into applause and cheers and demands for more. Danny Dunston was the show-stopping success of the evening.

The moral of the story, I suppose, is that you should never assume the worst is going to happen, or, more importantly, make premature judgements about people. However, when I tried to congratulate Danny Dunston on his performance, he cut me short.

'I used to do a bit of singing around the clubs, Johnny,' he explained. 'But I could never get anywhere with it. They told me I didn't have the right image for romantic ballads. I'm the wrong shape for a singer. They told me I looked more like a comedian. So I decided to become a comedian. But then they told me I wasn't good enough to do it professionally. So I gave up show business, and stuck to metal-bashing.'

I thought this was a rather sad story, but before I could dwell on it, Danny insisted on telling me the one about the drunken Italian farmer whose donkey fell into a ditch.

Which, now I bring it back to mind, was quite amusing.

La Dolce Vita

'What's your favourite place?' is one version of the question I am constantly asked. 'Where would you choose to go for your holiday?' is another.

It's not asked nowadays as much as it used to be when I appeared regularly on people's television screens, just as they were recovering from the excesses of Christmas and beginning to wonder where to go for their summer holiday – and, presumably, how to pay for it.

My colleagues and I had the job of showing them the world, providing them with choices, steering them towards best value for money, and doling out criticism – constructive criticism – when it was called for.

So the world and his wife assumed I knew everything about everywhere, would never make a bad holiday choice and, most important of all, had access to secret locations where I enjoyed holidays the like of which they could only dream.

This, of course, was far from the truth. And I would parry the question by saying that different destinations provided different delights, but all had their drawbacks.

If pressed, I would say that nothing could beat a long weekend in a British country house hotel, my favourite location being the Cotswolds.

But, when confronted by someone with real persistence, I sometimes had to admit to enjoying Italy. At which point those people would say: 'I guessed it. There's nowhere else like Italy.'

That is true. By the same token there is nowhere else like the USA or China. Nowhere exactly like Brisbane or Boulder, Lisbon or Liverpool. But, since you insist, I'll concentrate on Italy.

From the very start I realised that country would play a large role in my travelling life. I was young and crass and, of course, knew everything I needed to know when I first went there. Heavens, I even drank Campari and soda – a combination I now drink only before dinner on a cruise ship, and never ashore.

Fortunately I was in the company of an old hand, Arthur Eperon. I will save a full description for a different book – if I manage to get around to writing it – but Arthur was a great chap and a wonderful travelling companion. He was much older than me – but back then it seemed that everybody was.

So here we both are, in a small seaside resort near Alassio on the 'Riviera di Fiori', standing on a wide terrace overlooking the main square two floors below. I am clutching my Campari and soda. Arthur has a substantial glass of red wine. We are gazing down on the evening scene as we while away a little time before dinner.

The main square is chaotic. Café tables have spilled on to the road from the pavements, and are occupied by people having intense conversations, which involve much waving of arms and grand gestures. They are all drinking and smoking and oblivious to their surroundings. Meanwhile, traffic pours into the square from the narrow streets around it. Small cars, horns blaring, try to navigate their way from one side to another while avoiding the tables. Young men steer, and stall, their scooters. Their female pillion passengers sit side-saddle, displaying more shapely legs than are on show at the London Palladium.

A single policeman, waving white-gloved hands and constantly blowing a whistle, attempts to bring some sort of order to the scene. Naturally, nobody takes any notice of him. I won't attempt to describe the noise.

Having studied all this for a few moments, I sip my Campari and soda and remark, loftily: 'Italy would be a much better country if only the Italians could get themselves organised.'

Arthur looks at the lively scene, then at me. 'My dear boy,' he asks, 'what on earth makes you think the Italians aren't organised?'

✈

It took me many years to understand exactly what Arthur meant – years during which I have come to appreciate the many virtues of Italy and the Italians, not least their ability to outwit authority, ignore politicians and bend the rules.

If Italy has a grand purpose, it is to frustrate the bureaucrats of the European Union and make life as complicated as possible for the self-satisfied bean counters in Brussels as well as Rome. Italians are fully paid-up members of the awkward squad, questioning all forms of authority and setting an example to those of us in danger of being taken in by upstarts who would lord it over us if given half a chance.

Though there are aspects of Italy and the Italians that are deserving of criticism, anyone who does take a pop at that country and its people should bear in mind that, socially and politically, they've experienced just about everything.

Democracy, Fascism, anarchy. Kings, dictators, presidents. They have conquered, and been conquered in return. If any phrase sums up Italy and Italians it is, surely, 'Been there, done it, got the T-shirt.' And Italy has embraced all those systems with great enthusiasm before discarding them with equal vigour.

I am not a member of any political party, and hold strong views on very few topics, being content to live and let live, which I think pretty much sums up the attitude of most reasonable folk. But I do know incompetence when I see it. And propaganda. And blinkered insistence that the rules and rulers must not be questioned. Which is why I am glad Italy exists.

Italians have anarchy in their genes. If they achieve nothing else, their constant questioning of the rules and upsetting of carefully loaded apple carts is a good enough reason for their existence. We should follow their example, and strive to live La Dolce Vita – the good life.

Arthur had long ago learned that lesson, but was sensible enough not to explain it as we stood there on the terrace, knowing I would, in time, discover it for myself.

I had begun to appreciate how different Italy was when we drove along the coast towards France. Just short of the border we turned off the E80 (as it now is) and headed inland and upwards to Mortola Superiore, close to Ventimiglia. We were to lunch in a restaurant there, highly recommended by friends of Arthur who knew that he enjoyed his food almost as much as his wine.

We settled into our chairs as a waiter pushed a trolley towards us. It bore a selection of antipasti from which we were invited to choose. There was no menu and no option. But the food looked very good and we were happy to take our pick.

As the last of the antipasti was being consumed, another trolley appeared, with more tempting trifles. Again we chose, and again were more than satisfied.

And so it went on, trolley after trolley, each bearing more antipasti – more 'starters' – and each selection more tempting than the last.

After well over an hour we were absolutely full. The wines we had been served – not from a bottle, but a selection of glasses chosen to complement the different dishes – were as good as the food. But we knew when we were beaten and indicated our surrender by suggesting that a small coffee would be appreciated.

The waiter was taken aback. Were we not going to have a main course? But he smiled as he asked the question because he knew that nobody ever had a main course in that establishment. As for desserts, well, they kept a tiny selection in case of emergencies.

That meal – enjoyed well over fifty years ago – is as fresh in my memory as the day it was eaten.

Of course, it's not always been La Dolce Vita in Italy; and perhaps it's partly because of what the people have experienced that they have learned to enjoy life while they can.

Not so long ago, I was in the main square of Bracciano, a town on a hillside above a lake, some nineteen miles northwest of Rome, thinking about the Etruscans.

After the ancient city of Troy had fallen – thanks to that underhand manoeuvre with the wooden horse – a bunch of Trojans decided to skip town, seeking survival. Off they marched, roughly west by north, and ended up in what is today Tuscany, Umbria and Lazio. If the legend is to be believed, the twins Romulus and Remus, who founded Rome, were, in fact, two of those migrants from Troy who were to become known collectively as Etruscans. DNA tests on some folk living in that region of Italy, and similar tests on people living in Anatolia, that part of Turkey where Troy was located, have established a definite link.

Bracciano has the sort of square where, in the words of the oldest of travel writing clichés, one 'sits and watches the world go by'. But this time I did not sit, deciding instead to inspect that tiny corner of the world more closely. I walked across the square to the memorial which lists the local men who died in the First World War.

Spike Milligan observed that these memorials prove that, in war, people die in alphabetical order – a piece of nonsense which always springs into my mind when I am confronted by such monuments.

Sure enough the names were listed alphabetically. At the bottom were the Zavellonis – Remo and Romolo. Certainly brothers, possibly twins; and descendants of those Trojans.

They must have been young men when they died; young men with long lives ahead of them – young men whose potential was to remain unfulfilled. They had parents who grieved for them, and maybe siblings. Possibly wives; certainly girlfriends. When I recall my visit to Bracciano I cannot get the tragedy of their deaths out of my thoughts. On that warm September afternoon, it felt good to be alive.

✈

A few years after that first trip, I was back in Italy to see the resorts of Rimini and Lido di Jesolo. I had not planned to visit both on the same trip, but that's the way it worked out.

Rimini was something of a shock to the senses. I had visited plenty of seaside resorts, but the sheer scale of those along that particular stretch of Italy's coastline – the Adriatic Riviera – had to be seen to be believed.

Mile after mile of regimented sunbeds with attendant beach umbrellas planted from one horizon to another in rigid ranks. Behind them, hundreds of hotels lined the beachfront. And, behind them, more hotels and restaurants and bars and nightclubs. If ever a part of the world was totally devoted to the industry of holidaymaking, this was certainly it. I visited several resorts along that coast, but Rimini was head and suntanned shoulders above the others.

And it was there that I experienced the Italian ability to find an excuse for celebration at the drop of a hat, or, in this case, the wielding of a paint brush.

I had arrived in Rimini, you see, exactly when the annual Beach Umbrella Painting Competition was being staged. It was purely by chance. Thank goodness for serendipity.

My hosts explained the situation in considerable detail – which, you'll be pleased to know, I have largely forgotten. All I do recall is that every year artists were invited to design a beach umbrella. The one judged to be the best – and, naturally, the judging panel were major film and television celebrities of the time – would be the resort's official design for the following season and would be manufactured in huge numbers. There was a cash prize which came to several million lire, though competitors insisted they were entering for the prestige and honour of winning, not the cold hard cash.

So far, so straightforward. However, the actual staging of the competition was typically Italian.

Some two or three dozen huge umbrellas were lined up on the beach in front of one of Rimini's top hotels, undecorated and fully open, providing a canvas for each artist. The competitors were expected to work from stepladders while the judges observed their efforts from a balcony one floor above the action. I was on the balcony next to theirs, with a gaggle of local reporters and photographers.

Assistants were required to hold the stepladders in place. Other assistants had to fetch and carry brushes, paint, refreshment and whatever else was required for the creative process. That these assistants were overwhelmingly young and female and clad in bikinis added to the gaiety of the scene. So did the fact that each artist had a group of fans yelling their support, cheering, clapping and consuming large quantities of wine. As were the artists. And the judges. It was a fine example of creating something out of nothing. A fine example of how Italians can find enjoyment in the slightest of things. And, boy, did they enjoy it.

Some designs were abstract, others portrayed recognisable aspects of a beach holiday – starfish and sailing boats and palm trees. The judges pondered and discussed each one's merits. Their decision was announced with magnificent flourishes, and greeted with cheers and jeers. Then everyone retired to restaurants and bars to drown their disappointment or celebrate the success of the artists they supported. It was quite pointless, of course, but quite unforgettable.

The following morning a chum of mine named Jeffrey Rayner collected me from my hotel. Back in London he had asked if I would have the time to visit Lido di Jesolo, for which he was doing public relations work. As he was going to be there for a special event, he offered to drive me from one resort to another – a long journey, which would take most of the day, leaving around ten in the morning and getting to Jesolo around tea time. But it was one he was quite happy to make, as was I.

The event was another competition – this time to select Miss Cinema Europe. Aspiring young film actresses were invited to attend and have their potential assessed by a panel of experts in the field. It was, I think, just a variation on an old-fashioned beauty contest, but it did have the merit of requiring entrants to have appeared in a couple of films to establish their bona fides. A dozen or more hopeful young ladies had travelled to the resort from several countries, all accompanied by their mothers. The girls were very pretty. The mothers very formidable.

Now I had nothing whatever to do with this shindig, but one of the judges had yet to arrive and that judge was known to be 'a famous English journalist'. I was by no means famous, but I was certainly an English journalist and this fact registered with the girls – and their mums. They assumed I was the tardy judge and my protests that this was not so served only to reinforce their assumption. I found myself much in demand at the various lunches and dinners. Mothers smiled at me and positively encouraged me to talk to their daughters, even trot them around the dance floor when appropriate. I have never before or since been as popular among the fair sex.

It could not last, of course. The real 'famous English journalist' turned up three days later. She was Dilys Powell, *The Sunday Times'* legendary film critic. I was forced to flee from Lido di Jesolo.

No, that's not strictly true, because my trip had come to an end and I had to fly back to London from nearby Venice, anyway. But I couldn't do so without running a gauntlet of disgruntled mothers expressing their opinions of me in several languages which needed no translation. I like to think their daughters were less annoyed, but I am kidding myself.

So Jeffrey and I went to Venice, where we had almost three hours to wait before our flight. I had never been to that lovely city, so Jeffrey offered to give me a sightseeing tour. I thought about this, but declined.

'I don't want my first impressions of Venice to be gathered in a rush,' I explained. 'I shall come back with much more time to spare to properly appreciate the place.'

Jeffrey saw my point, so we spent most of our time having lunch in a restaurant frequented by tour bus drivers and guides – who always know the best places.

I did return to Venice later the same year. And I have visited it very many times since. But I shan't write about it now. I don't have enough time to do it justice…

Terminal Confusion

This tale is intended to be the literary equivalent of one of those little sorbets they give you when you are having a meal in a posh restaurant. Something to tickle the palate and give you cause to pause before going on to a more substantial dish. As the incident occurred in Athens, and I have used a restaurant analogy, I had hoped to work in a reference to the 'four course menu of the Acropolis', but can see no easy way of doing so…

So come with me to Athens airport. Not the Athens airport of today, which is reasonably decent as airports go, but to the one we had to use years ago. The one that was immensely inconvenient, as it had been designed to meet the needs of Olympic Airways rather than the travelling public in general.

If you arrived on an internal flight from one of the islands, which is what we had done, you then had to get yourself and your luggage to the international terminal. This entailed a very long journey around the outside of the airport, and usually meant you missed your connection.

And if, like us, you had a lot of filming equipment in addition to your personal bags, there was an extra hassle with Customs.

It was far from convenient. But in those days, nothing about Greece was convenient. And even then, nothing about Greece seemed to obey the rules that applied everywhere else.

So here you are, sitting with me and Tom, Robin and Roy. We have somehow managed to get from the Domestic to the International

Terminal, checked in for our flights, handing over personal bags and technical boxes after a Grade I haggle with the Customs' men, and gone through what passes for the security check to get to the departure lounge.

In those far off days, Athens airport security was a joke. Because, you see, once you had gone through it and were cleared to board your flight, you had time to visit the souvenir shops, some of which sold really big, ornately decorated daggers which would come in very handy should you and your chums wish to persuade a pilot to fly you to somewhere only you wanted to go.

On this particular occasion, however, the usual chaos was enlivened by the presence of a film crew from one of the local television stations, who were using the departure lounge to record sequences for what seemed to be the Greek equivalent of *The Bill*. Two or three actors were being filmed as they chased after two or three others, accompanied by a posse of lesser actors dressed as policemen. They ran this way and that, several times. At one point they all rushed up a flight of steps to a fake bar that had been set up on a landing for no other purpose than to have its stools and tables knocked over by the passing plod.

When the actors stopped for a rest – which they did frequently – passengers who had only just arrived, and didn't know what was going on, climbed the stairs to get a drink at the fake bar and got annoyed when they were turned away.

So they complained to the police – who happened to be actors dressed as policemen – and couldn't understand why this didn't get them anywhere.

It was anarchy on a truly Grecian scale, but the best part came when our detective heroes chased the villains into the gents' toilet. Now, at this point any sensible film director would have called a wrap and shot the next bit back in a studio, in a set constructed to look like a gents' toilet. But not these guys. They lugged the cameras and lights and sound equipment into the toilet and set everything up for the 'jumping on the villains, wrestling them to the ground and arresting them' sequence.

It was at this point we all decided we needed to go to the toilet, because – as our cameraman pointed out – what they were trying to do was impossible and it would be fun watching them as they realised this.

So in we went to find the Greek cameraman throwing a serious wobbly because there were large mirrors on every wall, reflecting him and his camera and the rest of the crew and their equipment. It was impossible to get a clear shot, which is exactly what our own cameraman had guessed would happen.

The director started yelling at everybody, including those of us who weren't working for him. So we yelled back.

Then a man dressed as a policeman came in, so the director turned his attention and his yells on to him – presumably on the grounds that he wasn't needed in this scene, was cluttering up the place, and should clear off and finish his tea break.

Unfortunately for him, this chap wasn't an actor dressed as a policeman, but a real policeman who'd come to find out why a crowd of men, desperate for a wee, were milling about outside the toilet, complaining that they couldn't get in.

There was a lot of screaming after that. So we tiptoed away to catch our flight to London.

As we climbed up the aircraft steps, brandishing our huge ornamental daggers, we decided that maybe Athens airport wasn't such a bad place after all.

Hump – or Chump?

Aside from folklore, funny food and hotels which don't live up to expectations, another occupational hazard for the travel journalist is encountering animals which end up being featured in one's articles or television programmes.

To begin, there was the rather magnificent snake, encountered in Jemaa el Fna square in Marrakesh. Or rather, the splendid chap who was charming him – and the watching crowd.

According to Moroccan legend, Jemaa el Fna is where we shall all gather on Judgement Day for the grand separation of saints from sinners. I think the Bible says something about dividing the sheep from the goats, a phrase I thought rather silly when I first came across it as a child. After all, I knew what sheep and goats looked like, and that there was absolutely no way of confusing one with another. Then I finally went to North Africa and saw sheep and goats that could have been twins en masse. So the job of sorting them could be tricky, whether it takes place in Jemaa el Fna or anywhere else.

Anyway, that's a digression, for which I apologise. I must concentrate on the square, which every visitor to Marrakesh is urged to visit. But not until late in the evening when darkness has fallen and it has come fully to life.

Naphtha flare lamps hang above mobile stalls whose owners are selling all manner of foodstuffs and souvenirs. Chaps in broad brimmed hats and ornate costumes wander around ringing bells and selling water from huge goatskins – or, rather, charging tourists who want to take their photographs, because there's more money in that than flogging water. The square is thronged with storytellers and jugglers and acrobats and musicians. And, of course, tourists who saunter, open-mouthed, from one part of the great concourse to another. Once seen, never forgotten.

If you happen to be in Marrakesh making a film report for a television travel show, then you include the square as a matter of course. Which is what we were doing on a warm spring evening many years ago.

I did the usual 'haggling with stallholder' sequence, and the 'tasting funny food and finding it not bad at all' routine. I managed to persuade our young director that there was no need for a ride in a horse-drawn carriage, as everybody did that, and suggested we should concentrate instead on a particularly fine snake charmer – a man of presence and style who hammed it up as soon as he spotted the camera.

His minions were working the crowd, with small baskets to collect coins and notes, and the senior of these made a beeline for the young director. She gave him a smile, but it was not merely a smile he was after. So she gave him a small bundle of notes and received a grudging nod in return.

As we filmed the snake charmer, he was absolutely first class, seeming to know just what the cameraman wanted. He finished up holding the snake in the air as the cameraman moved in slowly for a close up.

When we, and he, had finished, I thought I should at least try to thank him for his co-operation, though my knowledge of Arabic is confined to 'please' and 'thank you' and a couple of other useful phrases.

To my astonishment, he spoke excellent English. To my even greater astonishment, he knew who we were. 'Is this for the BBC *Holiday* programme?' he asked.

I told him that it was, and asked how he came to know about us.

'Oh,' he said. 'I do a season every year in Blackpool, on the promenade near the Central Pier. Just three or four weeks in the summer, but it is worth it, and my wife thinks it is a wonderful place for a holiday.'

✈

The other snake story comes, appropriately, from India – though again, it concerns the man rather than the snake.

He was a wizened little scrap of a chap who latched on to us one afternoon when we were filming in the grounds of a rather grand hotel (at which we were not staying on account of the budget being on the tight side). Having somehow avoided the hotel's Sikh security guards, the little bloke kept pestering us to film his 'act'.

However, he wasn't a snake charmer. In addition to a cobra, which he carried inside a small canvas bag, he had a mongoose on a leash. The entertainment he provided was to drive a stake into the ground, tie the mongoose to it, then tip the cobra out of the bag so the mongoose could go for it, in the way that a mongoose naturally does.

We knew this would never make it to a British television screen, and tried to tell him so. But he was persistent and, when we stopped for a pot of tea and cucumber sandwiches (it was that kind of hotel), we agreed to let him show us what his mongoose could do.

He was overjoyed. Driving the stake into the ground and tying the leash to it, he started to undo the string around the neck of the canvas bag. The mongoose became agitated, knowing what was coming next as the man tipped the cobra out of the sack and on to the grass.

It was a very pathetic snake. Judging by the scars and marks on its body, it had gone quite a few rounds with the mongoose, and not fared well. There were even a couple of sticking plasters over the worst of its wounds.

We tried to tell the little chap that we could not film the performance but, driven by the prospect of a bundle of cash from a television crew, there was no stopping him. Unfortunately, in his haste and greed, he hadn't fixed the stake firmly and, as soon as the mongoose lunged, it flew out of the ground. The mongoose fell upon the cobra and, within a few seconds, the snake was dead.

It was, we decided, a merciful release.

The little man went berserk. He leaped up and down in fury, demanding compensation from us because it was our fault this had all happened. There was no arguing with him, so we didn't try. Instead we just sat calmly, eating our cucumber sandwiches until two huge Sikh guards appeared, picked him up and carried him, kicking and squealing, out of the grounds.

To this day I do not know whether to laugh or cry when I think of that incident.

$\rightarrow$

I have no such reservations when it comes to considering the camel, and the trouble it caused. Although, to be fair to the poor beast, the doctor was responsible rather than the camel.

What became known as 'The Camel Affair' began on a ship named *Pendennis Castle*, one of the Union-Castle fleet of lavender-hulled lovelies which sailed with clockwork precision from Southampton to South Africa, by way of the Atlantic Islands – I think it might have been 4 p.m. every Thursday, but can't be certain.

On that voyage I sat at the doctor's table, and enjoyed lively dinners in the company of him and my fellow passengers. An Irishman, the doctor had a fund of stories about life at sea, and seemed to be something of an expert on all manner of subjects. Which is where the trouble began.

On the evening before our arrival at Lanzarote, a few of us mentioned that we planned to go on the camel excursion. The animals were introduced to the island a few hundred years ago, presumably for a practical reason, but now do nothing other than carry tourists over part of its moon-like landscape.

The doctor hoped we would have a pleasant day. He then waxed lyrical about the camel, speaking of its noble nature, its leather and its milk and its all-round general usefulness. Then, almost as an afterthought, he remarked that the camel was unique in being the only quadruped that could not swim.

We expressed our disbelief, but he explained that the combination of long legs and a big hump affected the camel's centre of gravity and, immersed in any depth of water, it could not avoid turning upside down.

'In any case,' he added, 'as the camel was designed to survive in deserts, where water is virtually non-existent, nature has not programmed its brain for swimming.'

Next day the coach took us high into the hinterland, stopping where a handful of chaps were sitting at the roadside, each with a healthy crop of camels. With the minimum of fuss, we mounted the beasts and set off in procession for our sightseeing, though the landscape had little in the way of sights to be seen.

Actually, it is almost impossible to board a camel without fuss. They start in a recumbent position, so you can get into the saddle fairly easily, but the trouble comes when they stand up. Rather than being 'a horse designed by a committee', which is the standard description of this beast, I have to tell you that the bloke who came up with the Anglepoise lamp must have had something to do with the camel's creation. Just as you think it is fully erect, it somehow finds another yard of height, to set you bobbing precariously. In most North African countries – especially Egypt – this is the moment when the camel man darts forward to give a steadying hand to the ladies; a hand which somehow manages to find its way up their skirts. But I digress...

On our return, and while we were waiting for the bus to turn up, I got into conversation with one of the camel chaps and, after praising the beauty of the island and the stout-heartedness of its people, in particular those who owned camels, I asked him if his noble beasts could swim.

This was clearly not a concept that had ever crossed his mind. He thought for a moment then pointed out that, as we were a good 1,500 feet above sea level, the question had never arisen. He saw no reason why they should not be able to swim, but confessed that he could not swear to this.

At that moment one of the camels rose to its feet, stood absolutely still with stiff, quivering, legs and began roaring as if in great pain. Without a word the camel man got to his feet, picked up a rock about the size of a house brick, walked over to the camel, and hit him over the head. Hard.

The beast shook his damaged head and sank back down, apparently none the worse. The camel man returned and explained that, from time to time, male camels get into a state of sexual arousal that can only be assuaged by a female camel – or a large rock.

I returned home, filled with lots of camel knowledge, and incorporated it into an article I wrote for *The Times*, whose travel correspondent I then was. I did not mention the incident with the rock, but did include the bit about camels not being able to swim.

Within a couple of days the paper was swamped with letters from people who knew that camels are perfectly capable of swimming.

We had letters from zoos and circuses, and splenetic missives – a couple in green ink – from chaps who had served with the Camel Corps in Mesopotamia.

The general tenor of these letters was that I was a blithering idiot.

And gullible.

And I could not disagree.

However, I nurtured for many years the hope that I would encounter that particular ship's doctor again. I planned to hit him on the head with a rock – or, if none was handy on board, something equally substantial.

Hideaways

An encounter with one of my neighbours sparked off this essay. Returning from my usual trip to collect the morning newspaper, I met a chap I've nicknamed Tiptoes Charlie, though I know very well Charlie isn't his name. But he is a bit of a Charlie, if you get my drift, and he does tend to trip along rapidly, as if late for an appointment, rather like the White Rabbit but without the pocket watch or the long furry ears.

I don't see him very often, but when I do he expresses surprise that I am not off on one of my trips to some exotic corner of the globe. As far as he's concerned, life for me is one long, jolly holiday. A lot of people think that, and I long ago gave up trying to tell them differently.

But on this particular morning, he also commented on a story in the newspaper about a chap who had escaped from custody when being transferred between prison and court. He'd spent a couple of weeks hiding out before being recaptured. As far as I could tell, he'd gone to ground in some thick woodland, built himself a hide, and presumably planned to live off the land until the hue and cry died down. Unfortunately for him, his idea of 'living off the land' meant pinching food from the big bins behind the nearest Tesco. He was spotted in the car park, chased into the woods, and promptly nabbed.

Charlie's point was that, having travelled all over the world, I must know some really good places in which to hide. In the highly unlikely event that I wished to avoid the attention of the Boys in Blue, a bit of woodland close to Tesco's would not be my first option. Which is why I found myself sitting at the desk thinking about hideaways, and places I have visited that would be ideal if one wanted to drop out of sight for a while. Although, in this age of instant communication, and with a camera on every mobile phone, I fear real hideaways are scarce and none of those I recall would suffice today. There was an island in the middle of the Kagera River in Uganda, where Toni Nutti, a Florentine lady, tiny as a terrier and hard as nails, ran a modest guest house. The meat course at dinner was most likely to have been shot by her that morning, and a hippopotamus named Hornblower walked the lawns, munching moonflowers and cabbages thrown out by the cook.

'He is called Hornblower because my husband used to read all those sailor stories,' she explained. 'He is not really tame, and I tell the cook to stop feeding him. But he takes no notice.'

Did Hornblower present any danger? She pondered my question for a moment and said he did not, unless you got between him and the water, in which circumstance he would become nervous and chase you and bite off your bottom. When you are on a small island, it is extremely easy to get between a hippopotamus and the water without intending to, so I walked carefully all the time I was there. With extremely nervous, tightly clenched buttocks.

A few months before I came to that island, in the year Uganda gained its independence, Toni's husband had been killed by a lone rogue buffalo. 'I cried for him,' she said one evening as we sat on the veranda, watching the sun go down and demolishing a second bottle of wine. 'I grieved for him. Then I decided I must do three things. Bury my husband. Kill the bloody buffalo. And get on with the rest of my life.' She had accomplished the first two and was working on the third with immense zeal when I turned up for my brief visit.

Yes, Toni's island would make a perfect hideaway – but it would have to be the place it was then, not the place it is now. The grotesque horror of Idi Amin was yet to come.

I also thought about 'The End of the World Club' in the frontier town of Eilat in the far south of Israel. There, the man who looked after the hotel motor boats was celebrating his marriage to the very pregnant cook, and their wedding guests, of whom I was one, drank and sang and even danced deep underground in something that must have started life as a simple cellar, but got out of hand. The End of the World Club, you see, was a full-sized night club, with a dance floor and a long bar and space for tables and chairs and even a band stand. Because I over-indulged in alcohol at the wedding reception, saying things I did not really mean – but, worse, not realising I was saying them – I was roused from deep sleep in the small hours of the following morning to be taken on a journey along the border by an Israeli army patrol. I am never at ease in the presence of men with guns, and my early-morning chums, who had seemed the jolliest of companions the previous evening, had transformed into humourless types who took things far more seriously than hitherto.

I resolved that I would never again drink alcohol at a wedding reception, and wax lyrical at length on the wonders of the desert, Lawrence of Arabia, and how the wide open spaces had a visceral appeal to all red-blooded Englishmen. You see, those lads had been among the guests who had listened politely to the ramblings of the drunken English journalist, about his wish to be at one with nature, to come face to face with the soul of the mighty desert.

And they had, equally drunkenly, promised to grant my wish. So Eilat would be on my hideaway list, so long as I remembered not to get drunk and boastful. But it would have to be the Eilat of then and not the Eilat of today, after war and with the threat of war.

✈

Not so the terrain just above the Cross Mill Iron ranch, in the Wind River valley of Wyoming, USA; that stretch where the trees start to thin out and great outcrops of rock dominate the landscape. There, between the woods and the many caves and tunnels in the rocks, I reckon I could evade the world for a spell. I'd have to get supplies from Burris, the nearest town, though between ourselves it's not so much a town as a crossroads with pretensions.

I couldn't raid the ranch because I have too much respect for the Miller family who owned it back then when I stayed as their guest and listened to their stories about the Hole in the Wall gang whose leading lights were Butch Cassidy and the Sundance Kid. A lot of people think the pair were fictitious characters, but they were real enough. Larry Miller remembered them from his childhood, and the trouble they got into. He and local people talked about their exploits as if it had all happened just the day before yesterday. And they told me how the famous film got it completely wrong.

The pair did not die in a South American shoot-out, but returned to Wyoming for a spell. A dozen people, including God-fearing Larry Miller himself, would swear on a stack of Bibles that they'd seen Cassidy around Burris long after he was supposed to be dead. Well, if he could get away with it, with a price on his head, maybe a nondescript dude from England might also succeed.

('What exactly is a dude?' I asked Larry one morning. He thought for a moment before replying: 'Someone from back east who knows nothing about horses and suchlike.' 'Would I be a dude, then,' I wondered, 'coming from England as I do?' He pondered again. 'Hell, John, of course you're a dude. If you came from anywhere further east, you'd be west.')

But my ideal bolthole, I think, would not be on Toni Nutti's island, in the resort of Eilat, or in the hills above the Cross Mill Iron ranch. It would be a town called Olbia. But, as with all the other places, it would have to be Olbia as it was when I first went there, not the Olbia of today.

I found that old Olbia up in the top right-hand corner of Sardinia, lying under the blazing sunshine and, as the brochure then put it, 'contemplating its bustly harbour or looking with nervousness towards the banditted hills.' The brochure went on to declare that visitors 'would likely be at Olbia in error'.

I arrived at Olbia one sizzling July afternoon on a railway train whose ancient engine wandered its way through those aforementioned hills along a winding single track, reached the town by the skin of its steam and flopped, panting with exhaustion, in the station.

'*Parlez-vous français?*' I asked the young man in the tourist office when it became clear that his English was as non-existent as my Italian then was. He did, so we parlayed for several minutes and I could tell there was more than a barrier of language between us.

Antonello read my letter of introduction for the fifth time. There was a long pause and silence, save for the slow beating of the ceiling fan and the shrill cries of some boys at play in the dusty alley.

'*Il-y-a un* Jolly Hotel…' I said at last. '*Je voudrais…*'

A slow shake of the head. The Jolly Hotel was full. So were the others in Olbia. Antonello shuffled with embarrassment. Some confusion caused by the non-arrival of letters from head office in Sassari. His boss away in Rome. Did I understand?

I understood. No rooms at the various inns. And no transport out of town until tomorrow. Suddenly I loathed all Italians, and their postal systems, and their fully booked hotels, and their tourist offices, and...

'Good afternoon,' said a voice from the doorway.

Antonello beamed with delight and relief. He spat out a burst of Italian, grabbed the newcomer and propelled him towards me. I shook hands, was ushered out of the office and within seconds was walking with the two of them up the shady side of the alley towards the Corso Umberto. Then, the Corso Umberto was Olbia's main street. Well, actually, it was just about the only real street that went anywhere. All the others performed gyrations around it, dodging round houses and under washing lines, through hen-strewn courtyards and back to the Corso again.

The newcomer, in perfect English, said: 'We shall take coffee, I think. Then we shall solve your problem.'

I asked who he was, as we crossed the square to the café of Signora Secchi.

'I am Spiro Kalantzes, and I come from the island of Corfu,' he replied. 'My father is a maker of fine wine. In our bottles we use cork from Sardinia. I am responsible for buying the cork.'

So we sat in the café of Signora Secchi and drank our coffee. Then, with Spiro as interpreter, we set out to solve my problem.

The solution came fast. A room in a private house could be obtained. Did I mind? I did not, and the boys from the alley, who had trailed us to the café in the hope of a cream cake from Antonello, were sent back to the tourist office to collect my suitcase and carry it off to the house he had in mind.

The house was a gem. In one of those meandering back streets, it had a huge courtyard floored with marble and set about with tubs of blue hydrangeas. A widow owned it, living there with her daughter, who was also recently bereaved. Antonello, via Spiro, asked if I minded being in a house with two widows. He seemed to think it was bad luck of some kind. I said I did not mind, and the pair of them showed me to my room.

The business of payment was arranged swiftly and with discreet dignity. I then expressed my sadness at the recent death of the son-in-law of the old *signora*, the husband of the young *signora*, and all this was gravely conveyed by Spiro. Then he and Antonello said farewell, promising to meet later in the café so we might discuss the island of Sardinia, the municipality of Olbia, tourism and other weighty matters.

And so began the finest fortnight I can remember from those long-ago days when I travelled alone. In a town I did not know, among people whose language I did not then speak (Spiro returned to Corfu two days later), I somehow became less of a stranger.

The thought that a *giornalista inglese* should find their town of interest both amused and flattered the Olbians – for this was years before the developers moved in, pushing up land prices, upsetting family structures, and raising villas and hopes and barriers of antagonism. This was long before the Aga Khan and his crowd created the playground for the super-rich that they christened the Costa Smeralda, with its expensive hotels and marinas.

Each morning I wandered out of the little house and up to Signora Secchi's café, whose wall clock gave me the first indication of time, for my watch was broken and the house of the widows seemed to possess no clocks at all. I'd ask for a coffee and pick out a plate of buns, and Signora Secchi would, for a few moments, regard me as her own – a kind of morning cabaret for the entertainment of her regular customers.

She smiled when I tried to read the newspaper, knowing I was trying to acquire a simple vocabulary, but was happy enough when I said 'please' and 'thank you' in Italian, and mastered a few other words and phrases. Nobody knew I had a phrase book in my case, and was studying it in the white-walled bedroom of the cool house, lying on the creaking double bed with its black iron frame topped with wobbly brass globes, invigilated by a soulful Jesus in a wooden picture frame.

The two *signoras* seemed to spend all their time in the kitchen, and each evening offered a meal which I accepted gratefully. Sitting in the kitchen with them, smiling and nodding when my sparse vocabulary failed, I was shown photograph albums, and framed certificates which meant nothing to me, but were clearly of great importance, judging by the way they were dusted before being handed over, and dusted again before being replaced on the shelf, or into the glass fronted cupboard from which they had been taken.

One day, with Antonello and a few friends, I was taken in a battered blue Fiat down the coastline to a favourite bathing beach. Two men, bent beneath the sun, with dust streaking their bare and sweating backs, were building a wall across the track which led down to the shore. There was an argument, a waving of arms, a grudging explanation, a spitting of curses. Some rich foreigner, 'from Manchester in Britain' I was told, had bought an old farm building and the land around it. The beach was his now, private. Keep off.

With the others, I cursed the invading foreigners and that evening we all drank a great deal of cold beer at the tiny round tables outside the café in Olbia's main square. It was my last night, and I did not want to leave my new friends.

Yes, Olbia as it was then, and with its people as they were then, is a place I shall always remember, and the place to which I would run and hide if the need arose.

Next morning when I prepared to leave for the station, Antonello and the others came to the house, shook hands gravely and said solemn things I did not understand. The two widowed *signoras* stood beside the hydrangeas as I bade them farewell. The emotion of the moment was broken by the arrival of Signora Secchi who embraced me to her ample bosom and presented me with a bag of cream cakes for the journey. Then she cried.

And, in that rattletrap train, winding its tired way back through the 'banditted' hills, I too shed a few tears. Had I known what was going to happen to that small and unspoiled part of Sardinia, I would most likely have wept until my journey's end.

Footnote: One of the drawbacks of longevity, as far as tourism is concerned, is that one remembers places as they were before development came along. For me the Costa Smeralda is one such place, as is the Algarve coast of Portugal, and various locations in Spain, away from the Costas.

Somebody once remarked that in the equation of tourism, success nearly always equals failure. Attracted to a location because the brochures promise 'unspoiled beauty' or 'tranquillity', visitors find neither because their very presence has changed the dynamic. However, as far as most communities are concerned, tourist development is good because it creates jobs for a generation who aren't content to exist on subsistence farming, or fishing, as the generations before them have had to do. It can abolish poverty. It is with that in mind that hacks like me write about new destinations, hoping that visitors will provide work and wealth for people who have little of either. Sometimes – too often – it doesn't work out that way and the best paid jobs go to outsiders while the big money leeches away to foreign bank accounts. But there's nothing the travel writer can do about that. All we can do is find new places and hope tourism will improve the lot of their inhabitants.

Jenny Darling
a 'faction'

Though she was barely out of her teens, Jenny Darling had worked on board the cruise ship *Athos* for almost two years.

Her main job was to tap and high kick her way through twice-nightly routines in the show lounge, but, as is often the case on small ships, her daytime duties were varied. Depending on the hour, she was either 'that pretty little girl who runs the exercise class', 'that sweet little girl who checks out the library books' or 'that nice little girl who helps with the bingo'.

And that was Jenny's problem. The passengers – her audience, her public – thought of her as a 'little girl' and, worse, a 'pretty', 'sweet' or 'nice' one. When your ambition is to be a top-flight dancer on the West End or Broadway stage, the tough top end of the show business ladder, that's not the image you want.

Technically, you couldn't fault her stage work, and her shapely legs and trim figure were undeniable assets. 'A lot of talent, perfectly packaged,' is how Tim Thomson, the cruise director, put it when we sat watching a rehearsal in the show lounge one afternoon. The six dancers were polishing up a routine for that evening's performance – Caribbean Calypso or some such title, as I recall. 'There's no doubt she has the talent,' said Tim, whose judgement was based on a career as an entertainer himself, as well as many years at sea. 'But the problem is that she moves as if she was still at Mrs Flora Ponsonby's Dancing Academy. She's got no oomph, if you know what I mean.'

I knew. *If you've got it, flaunt it* is an old show business maxim, but Jenny wasn't a flaunter, and Tim knew that would hold her back. The West End and Broadway would never be at her twinkling feet unless she learned to show herself off to better advantage.

What made the situation hard to understand was that Jenny was no shrinking violet, and was actually engaged in an affair with Captain Kyprianos, the 'old man' himself.

They had been involved in what Tim called a 'close personal relationship' for many months, in spite of the fact that Jenny knew the Captain was married, and that most shipboard affairs end in tears.

Most of us on *Athos* accepted the situation. Tim's sole concern was that Jenny might end up squandering her undoubted talent because of her emotional entanglement. I left the ship at the end of that cruise, but several weeks later was asked to step into the breach when one of the regular lecturers fell ill. I was able to rearrange a couple of other commitments and fly to Naples where the ship had called on the third or fourth day of her voyage. I was looking forward to seeing old friends.

Within half an hour of stowing my gear and reporting to Tim, I learned that Captain Kyprianos' wife and her mother were on board, taking advantage of the complimentary cruise granted each year by the shipping company to the families of their senior officers. Their presence meant, obviously, that the 'close personal relationship' between Jenny and the captain had to be suspended, and all who knew of it were required to keep their knowledge from the captain's lady and her mother.

They were a formidable pair. Mum was squat and shapeless and looked not unlike a well-lagged boiler as she waddled about the decks. She had a ferocious profile and this had been inherited by her daughter, along with the extraneous facial hair and solid shape.

Without in any way condoning his behaviour, one could understand why Captain Kyprianos had dallied dangerously with a dancer.

Jenny was taking the situation badly. Belinda, one of the other dancers, told Tim she spent most of her free time in their cabin, either crying or furiously vowing vengeance on the man who had done her wrong. I thought this was unfair, but long ago gave up trying to fathom the logic of female argument. All I knew was that it would be terribly difficult to keep the secret for the duration of the cruise.

The worst time was when the captain, accompanied by his wife and mother-in-law, entered the show lounge for each evening's second performance. A low table, with three chairs, had been reserved for them at the very front of the audience, so they could enjoy Caribbean Calypso, Way Out West, Hollywood Highlights or whatever musical montage was on offer, as well as the comedian, the magician, the ventriloquist and other star turns.

The passengers, almost 100 per cent British, loved every minute. However, I sensed that the captain did not, especially when Jenny and the girls were on stage.

One afternoon, a morose Jenny appeared in a corner of the forward lounge where we had gathered, as was our habit, for coffee and a gossip – 'we' being members of the Cruise Director's staff, the entertainers and the two girls from the ship's shop. Jenny filled a spare cup from the pot, plonked herself down beside Tim, and started talking about quitting the ship at the end of the trip, or as soon as she could get out of her contract.

Something drastic was called for. So I decided to stick my oar in and speak my mind.

'You are giving in far too easily,' I said. 'I don't give a damn about the rights and wrongs of this situation, or your relationship with Kyprianos, but having seen his wife, I can't help feeling sorry for the poor blighter. Whatever happens, he's stuck with her for the rest of his life. As for you, Jenny, I think it's time you showed him you're moving on from this affair. I also think it's time you showed him what he's losing.'

Tim caught my eye and smiled. He knew exactly what I was driving at, and stepped in smartly. 'Yes, Jenny,' he said. 'You've got it, so get out there and flaunt it. Goodness knows I've been telling you to do just that ever since you came on board.'

And that is precisely what happened that evening, and for every evening for the rest of the cruise. Jenny, who now had a reason to pull out all the stops, was a sensation. No more the sweet little girl from Flora Ponsonby's Dancing Academy, but a confident young woman aware of her talent – and her sensuality. She turned and twisted, kicked and dipped, swayed and shimmied in the finest display of flaunting it has ever been my pleasure to watch. I cannot swear to it, but I think I saw steam coming from the captain's collar. I certainly saw the grim look that came over Mrs Kyprianos' face, and the meaningful glances she exchanged with her mother. Poor man. Life would never be the same.

As for the newly transformed Jenny, she did eventually give up the shipboard life and hoofed her way around provincial theatres and on show tours around Europe and the Middle East. And though her name was never up in lights, she did make it to the West End.

I know this because I saw her in the chorus line of a Shaftesbury Avenue musical a couple of years later. I thought about leaving my card and a message at the stage door. But, remembering poor Captain Kyprianos, decided it was probably best not to do so.

Lobster at 30,000 Feet

In general, I am a trepid traveller by air. For one thing, I find it disconcerting to begin my journey while a young girl – who looks as if she was still in a gymslip this time last month – tells me about emergency exits and lifejackets under the seats and all the stuff that can go wrong. I also wonder who decided we should have access to lifejackets rather than parachutes.

I always pay particular attention to the thing the cabin crew do about exits and seat belts and oxygen masks, waving their arms about in theatrical fashion – if only to see how carefully they avoid eye contact with the passengers. Often frequent flyers know it by heart and don't listen, which leads some cabin crew members to inject extra comments to shake us from our indifference. On an internal flight in the USA, years ago, the girl was doing the routine about the oxygen masks dropping from the ceiling, concluding with the bit about 'if you are travelling with a small child, fasten your own mask before helping the child...'

Then, with a sweet smile, she added: 'And if you're travelling with more than one small child, you'll just have to choose a favourite.'

That made everybody sit up, as did the comment by the EasyJet lass – in broad Geordie – on a flight from Edinburgh to London. It was an evening take-off so she told us, as we taxied away from the stand, that the cabin lights would be dimmed.

'This is in accordance with normal practice,' she intoned. 'But on behalf of the cabin crew, I would respectfully request that male passengers keep their hands to themselves.'

My very first flight was in an Avro Anson, one Wednesday afternoon in the summer of 1954. I was in the RAF at the time, stationed at White Waltham, near Maidenhead. I was not a pilot, or indeed any kind of aircrew. However, a lot of chaps who were, but who found themselves promoted to desk jobs, used Wednesday afternoons as an opportunity to keep their hand in and clock up a few more flying hours.

Erks like me hung around the hangar, hoping somebody would offer us a ride, and to their credit these chaps were inclined to do so. You strapped on a parachute – pretending you knew how to use it – and off you went for a couple of hours. It made a nice change from the usual routine. Over a few months I sampled a lot of different aircraft – some of them quite small.

My first flight as a travel journalist was in a Dan-Air 'Elizabethan' – a version of the Airspeed Ambassador. This was in 1961, and the destination was Majorca. In February of 1958 an identical aircraft, operated by BEA, had crashed while taking off from Munich airport. On board were the Manchester United football team – the 'Busby babes' – as well as journalists and officials. That crash remained in the headlines for a very long time, and was at the back of my thoughts as I walked across the tarmac towards the steps.

Today a flight to Majorca is no big deal. Back then, the Elizabethan could not make it in one go. We stopped to refuel somewhere in the middle of France, and again in mainland Spain, finally arriving on Majorca after six or seven hours: as long as it takes to fly to New York nowadays.

I've already mentioned the DC3 that took me to Dubrovnik from Zagreb. Back then, the DC3 – the Dakota – was the workhorse of the European airline industry, just as its military version had been in the latter months of the Second World War. I imagine most of those civilian versions had seen wartime service, but we thought them almost glamorous. Well, we didn't have anything as a comparison, did we?

I once flew in a DC4 over the vast white wastes of Yukon Territory. It was a cargo plane, temporarily converted to carry passengers, and we sat in individual armchairs, fastened in place with lots of thick blue rope. There were sepia photographs of old aircraft on the bulkheads and, at the rear of the cabin, a coffee urn lashed firmly in place, just like the armchairs. Beside it was a large wicker basket containing chocolate bars and clingfilm-wrapped doorstep sandwiches. In-flight catering was a get-up-and-help-yourself affair.

In northern Ontario I flew with Bearskin Airways whose in-flight magazine had articles in English and the language of the indigenous First Nations, and lots of advertisements for heavy industrial plant and the sort of equipment lumberjacks need.

Some flights that did bother me were those we took within China during the course of a BBC filming trip in the 1970s. Until that time, tourism to China had been strictly controlled and was virtually non-existent as we understand tourism nowadays. The only way to get to China was as a member of a trade or professional group which had been invited by a similar group in China. So doctors and lawyers and architects and suchlike travelled with their spouses to undertake strictly controlled tours in the company of their Chinese opposite numbers. However, Cosmos made a breakthrough and featured China in their brochure.

The tour involved internal flights, operated by civilian aircraft but run by the Chinese Air Force – rather as if the RAF owned and ran EasyJet. (For the military to run a civilian airline was a strange concept which I encountered many years later when flying to the Galapagos Islands from mainland Ecuador.)

The planes they were using were old Russian jobs, bought for peanuts when Russia and China were bosom pals. However, the two nations had had a massive falling out, so the supply of new planes had dried up and spare parts were rapidly vanishing. The craft we flew in were, literally, held together with sticky tape – certainly the interiors were. Armrests had the habit of dropping off if you so much as stroked them, and bits kept falling down from underneath the luggage lockers.

We just had to hope the engines and wings were in better shape as we shuddered and juddered along the tarmac, heading for our take off. What made the situation even more interesting was the military pilots' attitude towards normal take off procedures.

The planes would get to the end of the runway, turn for take-off, rev up their engines – and take off. It did not matter that half the passengers were still standing up, trying to fit their cases into the luggage lockers. Or that the cabin crew were standing in the galley finishing their cigarettes. We were due to take off at a certain time, and Captain Courageous up front was determined that we should do so. Even if that meant people tumbling over and rolling along the aisles. Oh, happy days!

We were all terribly excited when jumbo jets made their appearance. They promised all manner of airborne luxuries, though for some reason decent leg room wasn't on the list – at least, not in the back of the bus. Shortly after their introduction, I flew to New York in a TWA Boeing 747. But not in the back of the bus. No, I was actually in First Class (there being no such thing as Business or Club Class back then).

In those early days the various airlines which operated the Boeing 747 were uncertain as to what they should do with the 'bubble' above the First Class section. Most had filled it with seats, but TWA had installed a restaurant: a proper restaurant with a handful of tables for four, laid out with crisp linen tablecloths and napkins, formal place settings and all the crystal and silver trimmings. When dinner time approached, we were invited to ascend the spiral staircase and take our seats. I was allocated a place at one of the tables. As the vodka and caviar first course was being served, I made the acquaintance of my fellow diners.

One was an oil man from Texas, who had been in London taking part in negotiations concerning his company's interests in the new North Sea oilfield. I never got his name, but remember he had a lot to say about British civil servants, none of it complimentary.

The second chap was named Fruehauf. At the time it didn't mean anything to me, but I later learned he was the chap whose name you spot on the back of large lorries when you are driving along motorways. He was quite old, and extremely rich.

My third companion was Walter Kissinger, older brother of the famous Henry – at that time US Secretary of State. He looked so much like him that they could have been twins. He talked of politics and political rumour.

Indeed, the talk flowed very freely. I said little, being aware that, compared with these three, I was barely out of childhood and had no experience of the world. But I listened, nodding sagely whenever I thought it appropriate to do so.

My cover was eventually blown. After the lobster, and the rare roast beef (carved on a trolley brought to the table, I'll have you know) and the impressive cheese board, not to mention the very fine wines, Mr Kissinger asked what I did for a living.

I should have lied. I should have hinted at inherited wealth, a decent-sized family estate in Shropshire or Somerset. Or spoken vaguely about being a writer, in such a way as to suggest learned academic tomes, or well-researched historical novels.

'I'm a journalist,' I said.

Clearly regretting every indiscreet remark they had made during our meal, my three companions decided to take their coffees in their seats, and scampered off down the spiral staircase.

On Gullibility

Having spent over half a century globetrotting at other people's expense, checking out holiday hotels, resort restaurants and nightlife, walking along the world's most blissful beaches and seeing its most spectacular sights, I can understand why people got the idea that life, for me, was one long holiday. It wasn't. The 'other people' who were footing the bills made sure they got their money's worth. There was little, if any, time for leisure on those working trips. Extensive notes had to be taken for the newspaper or magazine articles which were to be written, or the commentaries for the television reports. And with trips scheduled within days of each other, there was little time for leisure in between. Indeed, it is ironic that at the height of my career I was working far harder and longer than most, but because the end result – especially on television – portrayed the laid-back 'glamour' of travel and holidays, nobody believed it.

'Life's one long holiday for you, mate,' was the regular comment from friends and neighbours, taxi drivers and the like. So I gave up trying to convince them otherwise and went along with their fantasy.

It began in 1961 when I applied for a job which, as it turned out, nobody else wanted. That was to be the staff travel editor for a group of provincial newspapers. Subsequently I wrote for national newspapers and magazines, broadcast regularly on BBC radio and created a career in television.

And all the time I travelled – sometimes solo, sometimes with a small group of fellow writers, sometimes with a television crew. And sometimes with my wife and children.

With the passing of the years, I learned my craft. Learned to produce an article on time and to the length required. Learned to handle an hour of live radio. Learned to produce a film commentary that fitted its images. Learned to bear the pressure of a live television studio. And – most importantly – learned how to do it and make it look easy.

But it all took time...

In my early days I was as gullible as those ancient voyagers who believed foreign lands were populated by all manner of monsters in vaguely human form (medieval manuscripts and maps feature them heavily). And though I did not expect to encounter people who hopped about on one enormous foot, or had heads growing directly from their shoulders, or, for that matter, any dragons, I was gullible enough to fall into all sorts of modern travel traps.

First, there was the cliché of national stereotypes: Germans have no sense of humour, all Japanese are tiny, all Americans brash and all Frenchmen suave. And Swedes are all boring because, at heart, they are really plastic Germans. I'm sure you know the sort of thing I mean.

I've spent many an uproarious evening with Bavarians, laughing until my ribs ached – and, before you say anything, it had nothing to do with beer drinking. I encountered colossal Sumo wrestlers in Kyoto, many very sensitive people throughout the USA, and Frenchmen whose crassness astounds me still. I must admit that cracking Sweden's stereotype was a harder task, but I managed it one evening with the help of a vivacious female tour guide on the island of Gotland, a bunch of orchids picked from a meadow that afternoon and *Scheherazade* on the record player...

There are, though, aspects of travel – especially the kind of holiday travel about which I write – that are directly aimed at the gullible. Folk dancing is as good an example as any.

I was on the island of Sardinia just when development was beginning along what was to become known as the Costa Smeralda. A stretch of some twenty kilometres on the northeastern coast, it was developed by an international consortium headed by the Aga Khan. The project began in 1961, only a few months before my visit, but was to encompass – and greatly expand – locations like Porto Cervo, Capriccioli, Romazzino and Liscia di Vacca. Olbia was at its heart.

In one of the recently completed hotels, I encountered an American lady who was employed by an international hotel chain to travel the world creating 'ambiances' in their properties by the judicious use of lighting and colour. She was clearly good at it, but had chosen to take a holiday in a hotel that was definitely not one of 'hers'.

One evening, dining with her and half a dozen folk involved in the development of the area, the conversation turned to ways in which future guests could be entertained during their holidays. Good food and wine, comfortable accommodation and first-class service would go a long way towards keeping them happy, but we all knew that after a few days, holidaymakers require a boost to fend off boredom.

An obvious solution is to provide entertainment in the form of a local troupe of musicians and dancers (who, by travel writing custom, are always described as 'colourful'). Drawing on my experience of similar situations in the Caribbean, I made that suggestion. However, there was a major snag.

'We don't have any local music or dances,' explained a junior member of the management team. 'In this part of Sardinia, there are no such groups.'

To cut a long story reasonably short, the rest of that evening was spent inventing the required entertainment and over the course of the following weeks, long after I had returned to London, costumes were designed, dances choreographed and local folk recruited to put on the fictitious garb and perform the fictitious dances. The American lady was, apparently, the driving force, and arranged to stay on Sardinia to supervise the work instead of returning to her salaried role of ambiance creator.

A few years later I returned to the Costa Smeralda, though not to the same hotel.   Half way through my week-long stay a local troupe turned up one evening to play and dance and sing for us.

It was very well done, being, of course, 'colourful', as well as generally entertaining. My fellow guests certainly enjoyed it and discussed it with enthusiasm in the bar afterwards. I said nothing. Not even when the word 'authentic' was being bandied about.

Another example of catering to the gullible comes from Tunisia, specifically from the Hotel Les Orangers – which features, for other reasons, later in this collection. Way back then, Hammamet was a simple place; it was picturesque in all the ways you would expect a North African community to be, but the local people were disinclined to lay on any kind of show for hotel guests who opted to explore the place. They weren't being rude, but had no grasp of the concept of catering for the tourists.

One day, however, a German guest who happened to be a keen photographer returned from a visit to the nearby community, delighted at what he had encountered. And with every justification, as his trip had coincided with a wedding ceremony. He told the hotel manager how exciting it had been and, without realising it, planted a seed.

The following day the manager went into the village and had

long conversations with local folk. Three weeks later, guests at Les Orangers were informed they were fortunate to be in residence because, the following day, there would be a wedding in the town. On no account should they miss it. And on no account should they leave their cameras behind when they went off to see it, for it would be quite a spectacle.

From then on, the same couple got 'married' every couple of weeks. As guests stayed for two weeks at the most, this was a perfect arrangement. Only the villagers, the hotel staff and the tour companies' resident representatives knew the truth. And they, naturally, said nothing.

I am also reminded of an occasion when the cruise ship *Ocean Majesty* berthed at Honningsvåg, in north Norway, and we boarded the excursion buses for the trip to North Cape, the northernmost point of the European continent.

It was an impressive spot. High cliffs rose sheer from the heaving, slate grey sea. There was a monument – a large steel-mesh globe raised high on a metal stand and stone plinth – where tourists posed for photographs. A visitor centre provided a restaurant, shops and a small post office from which to send home specially franked postcards. There was a small exhibition gallery and historic centre and, of course, toilets.

Standing there, suitably impressed, I looked out towards the Barents Sea. And spotted another promontory which, though nothing like as impressive, was undeniably farther north.

'What is that?' I asked our local guide.

'That is Knivskjellodden Point,' he replied.

'It's farther north from here, isn't it?'

'It is.'

'So why do you bring the tourists here instead of there?'

'Because this is where they built the restaurant, the shops and the toilets.'

Food is another area of danger for the gullible, in particular that type of food known as the 'local speciality'. I have been gulled into tasting all manner of meals that would, in normal circumstances, never get within a mile of my knife and fork. Along with folkloric displays, the consumption of local specialities is one of a travel writer's greatest occupational hazards – some kind of fish soup with eyes staring up at you if you are visiting a coastal region, or some greyish coloured meat whose origin is best left unexplained, and a selection of vegetables you have never before encountered. Local people never eat the speciality of the region.

My greatest example of gullibility about local customs, however, comes from a press trip long ago to the island of Ibiza. The group included, among others, David Ash, then travel editor of *The Daily Express*, and a young lady from *The Daily Telegraph* who was not a member of their travel writing staff, but taking the trip as a 'perk'. I think it may have been her first foray abroad. She certainly knew nothing about Ibiza.

One morning, negotiating a flight of uneven concrete steps down to a beach, I noticed a small dog lying asleep on one of them, about half way down. I warned the others, who were following me, so they would avoid stepping on it. Instantly David asked: 'Is it a hurling hound?'

David, like me, had a particular (some might say peculiar) sense of humour. We were also very much on the same wavelength, so I replied that it was very likely to be a small hurler, but I thought islanders were no longer allowed to breed them.

The young lady from *The Daily Telegraph* hung on to our every word as we proceeded – over an excellent and well-lubricated lunch – to fashion a fantasy about the ancient sport of hound hurling, unique to the island, and how small dogs were specially bred to fit into the palm of the hand and be hurled out to sea, much as one hurls flat stones when playing ducks and drakes. Though the islanders knew from long experience that the dogs enjoyed it, interfering outsiders had caused the sport to be outlawed because of perceived cruelty, and the breeding of such dogs had also been banned. So the sight of this one was most unexpected.

We managed to keep straight faces as we embroidered our tale and, as far as David and I were concerned, it was nothing more than the sort of nonsense you indulge in when a trip becomes a little boring.

A couple of weeks later, at a press conference in London, I was buttonholed by a formidable lady named Alice Hope, a doyenne of the *Telegraph*'s travel writing staff. She was somewhat angry because her young lady had returned from Ibiza and written an article which included comments about the former pastime of Hound Hurling, its cruelty and its eventual banning. I do not know to this day whether Alice had managed to catch the story before it went to print. I like to think that it did see the light of day, however. Readers of a sober journal such as *The Daily Telegraph* deserve nothing less than the full story.

National Stereotypes

Some while back I mentioned that we'd be returning to the Hotel Les Orangers, in the Tunisian resort of Hammamet. And here we are. Well, almost. Bear with me a moment, as I set the scene.

You can't spend well over half a century travelling the world without realising that everybody has fixed ideas about how the citizens of different nations are likely to behave. We all fall prey to preconceptions, no matter what our nationality happens to be, though I have a feeling that the British in general, and the English in particular, are more prone to this than most. Though maybe that's a national stereotype in itself...

It could be a throwback to the time when we ruled an awful lot of the world and knew, without a shadow of a doubt, that an awful lot of the world was all the better for it. We had picked up what Rudyard Kipling called 'the white man's burden', and borne it to those far corners of the globe where people did not appreciate the importance of playing the game, dressing for dinner and passing the port to the left.

And in my opinion, an awful lot of the world did benefit from our presence. Those scallywags in the United States of America who rose up against us in 1775 would be far better off now if they hadn't won their War of Independence. For starters, they'd be playing a decent game like cricket – and quite likely being very good at it – instead of wasting their time on rounders. And they'd be driving on the proper side of the road. So there.

Anyway, for better or for worse we do tend to pigeonhole people according to their nationality, and, in that context, travel often narrows rather than broadens the mind, as people set out to reinforce the prejudices they have brought from home.

I can't recall who described Switzerland as an open-air branch of Barclays Bank, populated by head waiters, or that the personality of the aforementioned Swiss was exactly like their watches – precise but anti-magnetic. But, with apologies to the Swiss whom I have found to be generally decent types, those are examples of the prejudice I have in mind.

As, of course, is the classic description of Heaven being a place where the police are British, the chefs Italian, the mechanics German, the lovers French. And everything is organised by the Swiss.

Hell, however, has German policemen, British chefs, French mechanics and Swiss lovers. And is organised by the Italians.

The tendency towards a default attitude of suspicion when encountering foreigners is nothing new. Back in 1143 a monk named Aimery Picaud wrote probably the world's first guidebook, for pilgrims travelling to Santiago de Compostela. In it, he warned his readers to beware of innkeepers who might drug their drinks in order to rob or even murder them.

Six centuries later a chap named Philip Thicknesse wrote *A Year's Journey Through France and Part of Spain* for the benefit of his fellow Englishmen making the same journey. He advised them to include in their luggage a wedge or similar device for securing the door of their bedchamber, '… for visitors cannot take too much caution in a country where murder and robbery are synonymous terms…'

But back to this tendency towards stereotyping: assuming that every member of a particular nation will behave in a certain, 'typical' way.

Several years ago a press release from American Express crossed my desk. To gain publicity for their travellers' cheques, they had carried out a Europe-wide survey, asking people what most annoyed them when they were on holiday. Top of the hate list as far as Italians were concerned were people making too much noise. This, from probably the noisiest people in Europe, was, I thought, a bit much. However, the Germans took the proverbial biscuit by citing as their pet holiday hate – wait for it – people who reserved sun beds by putting towels on them!

Which, fortunately for both of us, brings me at last to the hotel in Hammamet. It was a good many years ago, and most of the hotel's guests were there on package holidays organised by a British firm named Clarksons and its German counterpart, Neckermann. The majority were of an age to have taken part in the Second World War. So I guess I don't have to spell out the general atmosphere around the place, or the air of tension that prevailed.

Each morning the Germans would rise early, place towels on the sun beds, then go in to breakfast.

The English, on the other hand, would take their breakfasts first, then amble out to the sun beds ranged around the swimming pool, throwing off the towels and reclining on the sun beds, as to the manner born.

When German guests turned up, arguing that this, that or the other sun bed was reserved, the reclining English lads and lasses would reply to the effect that bums, not towels, reserved sun beds. Grumbling, the Germans would retreat and occupy other recliners. But it was not an auspicious start to the day.

The ridiculous thing was that there were more than enough sun beds to go round, ranks and ranks of them, all around the pool on a wide, sun-drenched area. No one was in a more favourable position than any other. To reserve a particular sun bed was pointless. The hotel staff watched the morning confrontations with a mixture of disbelief and amusement. They probably thought it was all part of some strange, northern European ritual. Which it was.

Lunch was a buffet affair. Guests of both nations plunged in recklessly. There was no attempt at forming orderly lines, and an awful lot of shoving and sharp elbow work went on. The afternoons were spent in simmering resentment – and simmering in the sunshine, of course. One had the distinct feeling that both sides were preparing for the evening's hostilities. Or, at best, a hostile evening.

Dinner was a tense affair. And, as people were now drinking a lot of alcohol, I feared the worst, especially when guests retired to the bar to top up their restaurant consumption.

To my astonishment, however, the alcohol had a mollifying effect. English and German guests would actually start talking to each other (in English, of course, because every Englishman knows that his is the only language spoken wherever he chooses to go, and people of other nations are sensible enough to learn it).

Charlie would buy drinks for his new friends Hans and Greta, and Hans would buy drinks for Charlie and Doris. The men would reminisce about the battles they had fought and the friends they had lost. The women would sigh and even shed a few tears.

Then, arms round each other's shoulders, a wine-mellowed Hans would say: 'I tell you, Charlie, my son will never grow up to fight your son.'

And Charlie, just as mellowed, would reply: 'Bloody right, Hans. It's always us working blokes who get the worst of it.'

Doris and Greta would exchange understanding looks.

Then everybody would sing 'Lili Marlene' and stagger off to bed.

Next morning, the Germans would rise early, put towels on the sun beds, and go into breakfast. And the English…

Well, you know the rest.

The Flying Lesson

One of the unforgivable sins connected with working trips – apart from not buying the drinks when it is your turn – is to be late. It is unprofessional, and causes inconvenience to your colleagues who are working as hard as you, and quite possibly harder. On press trips, in addition to being prompt, it is simply not done to delay your companions by insisting on a 'photo stop' when everybody else is anxious to get back to the hotel at the end of a long and trying day.

As far as filming trips were concerned, the 'call rule' was a simple one. At the end of the working day and before everyone dispersed to follow their evening inclinations, the director would declare the following day's start or call time. And that was inviolable. If it was 7 a.m., it was 7 a.m., ready to go. Not 7 a.m., 'have I got time to grab a coffee or some breakfast' time. Not 7a.m., 'God my head is killing me, we'll have to stop off at a chemist' time. To be late was to be discourteous.

I know – but will not name – well-known television presenters who were hated by film crews because of their habitual tardiness. I even know of one who insisted that filming schedules be so arranged as to allow her an hour's nap after lunch.

However, it is another aspect of lateness that concerns me now: being so late as to miss the plane or the ferry in the first place.

In a lifetime of professional travelling I have only once ever missed a flight, and that was because a jolly Public Relations chap insisted on giving me a lift to London Airport (as Heathrow was then known), then further insisted that we had time for a couple of drinks in a pub *en route*. As we stood in the pub car park, with him searching vainly for his car keys (my case being locked in the boot), I realised I would not be going to the Isle of Man that day.

The only other time I missed my transport occurred during a hectic summer sometime in the 1970s. It was the afternoon ferry from Poole to Cherbourg. The BBC had organised a driver and car to transport me from my southeast London home to the ferry terminal. Unfortunately they had underestimated the time it would take, to say nothing of the amount of traffic on the A31. Suffice it to say that the car deposited me at the terminal just as the ferry was nosing past Sandbanks.

A young lady from the ferry company's press office was waiting to escort me to the communications room where a call was put in to the vessel. After a few moments, Tom, the director of the programme, came on the line; he and the rest of the crew were on the ferry. Under the circumstances, he was fairly calm. Fairly. Shorn of adjectives, his instruction was simply that I should get myself to Cherbourg with the minimum of delay. He couldn't wait around after the ferry's arrival.

If the worst came to the worst – and it looked very much as if it would – Robin, the sound recordist, would remain in Cherbourg with one of the cars and be responsible for getting himself and me down to the filming location. Messages would be left in the ferry company's office at Cherbourg, which would also be our rendezvous point; this was long before the advent of mobile telephones.

The ferry, I knew, would take a little over four-and-a-half hours to reach Cherbourg. No more ferries were leaving that day.

I raced out of the building, slung my case on to the back seat of a taxi and instructed the driver to get me, as fast as possible, to the nearest airport – Hurn, a little way north of Bournemouth.

At Hurn I learned that the last cross-Channel flight had long departed. Nothing was going out except for a flight to Jersey, leaving in fifteen minutes. Could I get on that? I could. And did.

We took off and set out across the Channel. I spotted the ferry far below, making its way to Cherbourg. I had no idea how I would proceed after Jersey, but at least I was geographically closer to my destination, which, I reasoned, had to be better than nothing.

The flight was uneventful, the landing reasonably good. I scampered into the terminal building, collected my case, and rushed to the inquiry desk.

How could I get to Cherbourg? Or, for that matter, anywhere in mainland France. Were there ferries from the harbour? Were there flights from the airport? In my anxiety I fear I may have raised my voice.

The smart lady behind the counter looked sternly at me. There were no ferries, she informed me. And no flights – nothing out of the airport except for flights to the UK – until the following morning. I looked at my watch. It was a little after 6 p.m. The ferry was due into Cherbourg at around 7.30 p.m.

I crumpled. Internally, that is. And quite possibly externally as well, because the smart lady's look softened perceptibly. 'What exactly is the problem?' she asked.

So I rattled out the whole story: the missed ferry, the hasty flight, the guilt at having let down my colleagues and, of course, the inability to let them know what was happening.

The smart lady sucked in air through her teeth, thought for a moment, then came to a decision. 'What you need,' she said, 'is a flying lesson.'

'What?'

'My husband is a pilot with Dan-Air,' she added. 'He's off duty at the moment, and at home. But he sometimes gives flying lessons, and I'm sure he would be available to give you one. Perhaps a flight in the general direction of Cherbourg might suit you?'

She reached for the telephone, spoke swiftly and crisply into it, then put down the receiver and told me to go and get a cup of coffee and a sandwich, as it would be at least ten minutes before her husband could collect me.

I did as I was told and was sitting patiently in the cafeteria when she strode over towards me, a tall chap at her side, grinning from ear to ear.

With the minimum of fuss, and certainly no waste of time, we established what my lesson would cost (extremely reasonable, under the circumstances) and I found myself being driven out to a corner of the airport where small planes were parked.

After I had completed a couple of forms – one of which, I believe, was a membership application for the Jersey Flying Club – we clambered into a Cessna and within a few minutes were airborne and heading towards Cherbourg. I sat beside him, watching the ease with which he handled the little craft.

'I am going to hand over the controls to you,' I heard him say through my headphones.

I looked at him, terror in my eyes, but he laughed. 'I am supposed to be giving you a flying lesson,' he said. 'So you need to take the controls.'

So I did, for what seemed a very long time, with him keeping a beady eye on me and the aircraft's instrument panel. Then, to my great relief, he signalled he would take back the controls.

As he did so, he radioed Cherbourg to tell them that he had a minor problem and requested permission to land in order to check it out. Permission was, of course, granted.

We landed and taxied off the runway and off out of sight behind a building. He cut the engine, got out of the plane and helped me descend, handing my bag to me as he did so. 'If you go through that gate,' he instructed, pointing to a gate in the fence a few yards away, 'you will find yourself near to the front of the airport main building. There are taxis there.'

I thanked him warmly and, lugging my bag, headed for the gate and the taxi rank. Fortunately there was a taxi – just one – outside the building. As no incoming flights were scheduled, I can only assume he was there to ferry home any traveller who had stayed too long in the bar, or perhaps members of the airport staff. He looked at me with great suspicion, but I was waving a bundle of francs in his direction, so he opened his door and ushered me in.

We set off along the road which winds downhill from the plateau towards Cherbourg and he asked me how I had come to arrive at such an unusual hour. I told him, as best I could in my schoolboy French, that I had had to collect my case from the hangar, because it had been left behind in error. Without actually saying so, I intimated that I had, of course, passed through all the proper Customs and Immigration formalities.

Then I made the mistake of explaining that my colleagues were crossing from England in the ferry, and I wanted to be there to meet them if possible.

He looked out towards the sea. It was a superb view from our height above the town.

'Do you mean that ferry?' he asked.

About a mile off shore, the ferry was heading for the harbour. 'Yes', I replied. 'That is the ferry.'

'Hold tight,' he said – or whatever 'hold tight' is in French.

Then he drove as only a French taxi driver can. The honour of the Cherbourg Taxi Drivers' Association, to say nothing of his personal honour and that of La Belle France, depended on him getting me to the disembarkation point before the ferry arrived.

We screeched and screamed down that road, darted through town traffic, and came to a juddering halt at the terminal gate. He indicated that all disembarking cars would pass that point. All I had to do was wait.

I paid him and gave him a tip which even he thought was excessive – but which he accepted with a conspiratorial smile, as I don't for a moment think he believed my story about how I came to be so late leaving the airport.

He roared off – probably to his favourite bar where he could buy drinks for his friends with my tip money, and tell them – as if they needed telling – what lunatics the English were.

A few minutes later I spotted Tom driving the first of our cars, with production assistant Prue in the front passenger seat. Their jaws dropped when they saw me, but he drove slowly past. As did Roy, the cameraman, with his assistant in car number two. Then came Robin in the third car. He stopped and watched in disbelief as I opened the rear door, threw in my case, then slid into the front seat beside him.

Behind us, horns began to blare.

As we started off, Robin said, simply: 'How?'

'I'll tell you later,' I replied. 'Have you re-tuned the car radio yet? We might still be able to get the BBC.'

Day Trip to Saint Lucia

For a number of years my wife and I used to take a brief holiday on the island of Barbados, basing ourselves in a small hotel called the Tamarind Cove – a beautiful conversion of what, I believe, had been an old plantation house or a sugar mill. It had bungalows dotted about its grounds, a tree growing through the roof of its poolside bar, and was what would be called nowadays a 'boutique' hotel. Unfortunately, nowadays it is far bigger and far less attractive, so I no longer go there.

One year our daughter Sarah joined us. The plan – if, indeed, there was a plan – was to take it easy, do some sightseeing in our hired Moke and generally have a pleasant time before returning to our respective rat races.

About three days into the break, the girls expressed a desire to take a trip to nearby St Lucia. I mentioned this to one of the staff behind the reception desk who said she knew someone who could help.

Early that evening a young man turned up at the Tamarind Cove. Joseph was a neat, orderly sort of chap, with an impressive briefcase and a business card which identified him as the representative of a fine-sounding travel company based in nearby Jamestown. As the card had only a couple of misprints on it, and as he seemed eager to do business, we began our negotiations.

If we wanted to purchase our day trip, he explained, a limousine would collect us from the hotel reception next morning and take us to the airport, where we would join the small but select band of trippers for the short flight to St Lucia on a specially-chartered aircraft. On St Lucia, a coach – a luxury coach, naturally – would take us on a tour of all the island's sights, pausing for us to enjoy a sumptuous lunch at a hotel called Le Toc.

The price quoted seemed pretty reasonable to me, so I handed over a deposit and promised that all three of us would be waiting in the reception area next morning.

The first indication that things might not go quite according to Joseph's plan was that, five minutes after the appointed time, he arrived in a somewhat battered VW van with a young man in dreadlocks draped over its steering wheel.

This friend of Joseph's had a big grin and was smoking what an acquaintance of mine once described as 'a Rastafarian Woodbine'. Joseph stumblingly apologised for his tardiness and the van, but the three of us sensed adventure in the air, so cheerfully clambered aboard. We simply wanted to head for the airport and discover just how this 'dream day' would pan out.

Once at the airport, and with the van disappearing in a cloud of dust and small pebbles, we established that we were the only passengers Joseph had managed to round up. And that, under the circumstances, he had not bothered to arrange for air transport – chartered or otherwise.

I'm sure he expected us to shout at him, demand the return of our deposit, and head back to the Tamarind Cove in high dudgeon – a chauffeur-driven dudgeon, of course. But we, and in particular my wife and daughter, were in the mood for a little excitement.

With Joseph in tow we headed to the desk of an air charter company where I negotiated the hire of a light aircraft and pilot. I was delighted – and relieved – to discover that American Express would 'do nicely'. I asked young Joseph if he would like to come with us; after all, this trip was his idea. He rummaged around in his briefcase, whimpering slightly, before coming up triumphant with his passport.

So we popped him into the back of the plane, popped my wife in the front beside the pilot, while my daughter and I occupied the two seats in the middle. We zipped smartly over to St Lucia, arranged a pick-up time with the pilot and, as he took off and headed back to Bridgetown airport, asked Joseph if he could point out the luxury touring coach he had promised.

Of course, he could not. But no matter, for a very large taxi was at hand with a driver who was willing to put himself and his vehicle at our disposal for as long as we needed him. I decided to let Joseph negotiate the price, as I felt it was time he contributed something to the day.

We set off, via a petrol station, and as time passed Joseph recovered his composure and started telling us about the sights we were seeing. Unfortunately, the taxi driver kept butting in with corrections, as he obviously knew far more about his island than did Joseph.

We saw a lot of sights, including a drive-in volcano, and, as promised, our route took us to the hotel Le Toc. We were not surprised when Joseph confessed that he had not actually made a booking for lunch. In any event, it was not a problem. Two days previously a fire had caused the kitchen to be closed and Le Toc was only able to serve cold salads, with a very small selection of barbecued beef, chicken or fish. Consequently, its dining room was deserted.

The hotel people were full of apologies, as if it was their fault. But apologies weren't needed. After all, who wants to eat a hot meal in a restaurant when one can sit outside on a shaded terrace with a fine view of the glittering Caribbean, a healthy salad, some grilled fish and a few cold beers?

By this time, we were getting very relaxed. Young Joseph said he felt 'adopted' by us. The taxi driver turned out to be a cricket fan, not surprisingly, and told inspiring stories of umpiring local school matches and nurturing the kind of talent that was, one day, going to demonstrate the worth of St Lucia at Lords, The Oval and Trent Bridge. We made our leisurely way back to the airport, arriving just as our plane swooped in to land. Sarah sat beside the pilot for the journey back. (Much later, she and her mother would agree that he was 'really dishy'.)

At Bridgetown, Joseph's friend was there with his battered van, his grin and his spliff, so we headed back to the Tamarind Cove where, to the displeasure of some of the American guests, I invited the pair of them into the bar for a couple of beers to celebrate an unforgettable day.

As we sat there, Joseph and I did some sums. The whole trip had actually cost me around $60 more than the very low price he had quoted when he had first appeared with his briefcase and his nervous enthusiasm. Over lunch at Le Toc he had, with unexpected grace and no little dignity, refunded me the deposit.

At the end of our calculations we agreed that, what with his free day out, his lunch at Le Toc, which I had paid for, and the two – no, make that four beers he and his friend were now enjoying, we were more or less quits.

As we waved the pair of them off, I saw young Joseph take a long pull at his friend's roll-up. He had had an eventful day.

So had we. However, when they heard our story, many of the American guests at the Tamarind Cove were shocked at the numerous ways in which we had been let down. Most of them said we ought to think about suing somebody. I didn't agree.

For one thing, I doubted that Joseph's fine sounding travel firm existed anywhere else but in his head and on his business cards. The chances of getting anything out of him were so small as to make any action a total waste of time and money. But there was a far more important reason. The fun we had had that day was beyond price. We had laughed ourselves silly time and time again, and increasingly enjoyed the company of Joseph and the St Lucian taxi driver as the barriers came down. The lunch at an otherwise deserted hotel was splendid, and the flights had been spectacular because the pilot had made it his business to ensure we saw the sights and the best of the islands' coastlines on the way out and home again.

At the end of a day crammed with unforgettable incidents, we sat on our balcony drinking chilled white wine and watching the pelicans diving into a shoal off fish just off shore. The huge, red sun dipped behind a thread of clouds above the western horizon.

No, that day we were in no mood to sue anybody. Indeed, our day had been so full of fun and incidents that we would happily have given young Joseph a five-star recommendation.

An Invitation to 'The Pig'
a 'faction'

S teve Turner ran a first class bar.

A cheerful, personable chap, he remembered names and faces, as well as his customers' preferences. He kept the conversation flowing, created a pleasant atmosphere and would have made a fortune in tips in any smart night club or hotel. But Steve Turner was not to be found in any hotel or night club. He plied his bartending skills afloat and, when I met him, was working very happily on board the *Ruritania*.

(Yes, I know. The *Ruritania* doesn't exist, but you'll understand why I cannot give you the ship's real name as my tale unfolds: a tale of late-blooming love, and how a man contrived to fall in with his wife's romantic wish and avoid the ensuing social embarrassment.)

It was Steve who first paid me the greatest compliment a passenger can be paid – greater, I dare suggest, than being seated at the captain's table. A couple of days after I had embarked at Naples he invited me to join him for a drink after his work was done. In the crew bar.

As on most ships, the bar was a little on the rough and ready side, but filled with good humour and friendship. Living cheek by jowl, as they do, crewmates learn to tolerate each other's fads and foibles. 'The Pig & Whistle' is where they unwind, and for a passenger to be invited to share that precious time in 'The Pig' is, as I said, the greatest accolade.

About eighteen months later, when a fellow writer mentioned that she would be sailing on *Ruritania*, I told her to look out for Steve and give him my good wishes. But she returned with news that Steve was no longer on board. His charm and banter, and maybe his nimble way with a cocktail shaker, had won the heart of a lady passenger. A mature, widowed lady, it has to be said. But, as he headed farther into his fifties, Steve reckoned that Vera Sutcliffe was the woman he'd been waiting for, and he decided to wait no longer. At the end of that summer, he signed off and went to Yorkshire, to wed Vera and spend the rest of his days running a small hotel near Skipton.

I didn't expect our paths to cross again, but when, five years later, I found myself back on *Ruritania*, there he was. As a passenger. And looking none too happy about it.

He explained why, after we had caught up on old times in a quiet corner of the sun deck.

'Vera and I were made for each other,' he said. 'We both love running the hotel – and you must come up and stay when you can – but she does have a hankering for this cruising lark.'

'And you don't?' I suggested.

'Oh, I don't mind,' he said. 'We've been on at least half a dozen cruises since we got wed. But until now I've managed to persuade her to go on other ships. Not the ship I used to work on. You see, they know me here.'

Instantly I realised his problem. As a passenger he would be meeting, on equal terms, officers to whom he was once subordinate. And the cabin and bar stewards and restaurant waiters were, for the most part, old friends who couldn't be ordered about. Steve would be navigating through a social minefield.

As the days passed, he made a brave show of enjoying himself and, indeed, I think he generally did. But it wasn't easy, especially as far as some of the junior officers were concerned. Their comments and their general demeanour, when they found themselves in his company, were as easy to read as a wide-open book. Indeed, one or two muttered about him not 'knowing his place', which, to my way of thinking, said more about their lack of social graces than his.

The senior officers did not appear at all concerned; as on most cruise ships, they mingled rarely with the majority of passengers, concentrating on those few who sat at their table in the restaurant. But there was no doubt that things were not running as smoothly as they should, as far as the junior officers' attitude towards Steve Turner was concerned. It was unfair, of course. Steve didn't deserve the slights and snubs, for he was making a great effort to fit into his changed circumstances.

After four or five days, I noticed that he was never to be seen around the ship after dinner. Vera was a gregarious and sociable lady, chatting away in the bars and lounges, taking part in the quizzes, attending the shows and generally having a good time. But of Steve there was no sign. Had he, I wondered, retired to their cabin to mope in solitary silence?

'Oh, I don't know what he gets up to,' said Vera when I broached the subject. 'We always tend to go our separate ways after dinner when we're cruising. We like to do different things, you see. He's not one for shows and quizzes and that sort of thing.'

This was no surprise, for I have encountered scores of couples who fall into that very same pattern of behaviour when cruising. Perhaps it is a testament to the strength of a marriage that a couple on a cruise holiday are as happy apart as they are together.

But Vera must have had a small cause for concern, because she added: 'Maybe coming on *Ruritania* was a mistake. I know Steve wasn't keen on it. But it's our fifth anniversary this year and I thought it would be romantic to return to where we met.'

I said nothing, but thought it a pity that a nice fellow like Steve should be having such a rotten time through no fault of his own. Clearly he could manage the days at sea by simply relaxing in the lounges, or on deck with a book or a beer. But the social side of evenings on *Ruritania* was obviously too much of a hurdle.

One afternoon, Tim Palmer, who'd taken over Steve's bar, asked if I would be his guest that evening for a few drinks in 'The Pig'. As always, I was flattered and honoured, and accepted without hesitation.

And that's where I found Steve Turner.

In contrast to the attitude of those junior officers, his old shipmates were showing their respect and affection for him. During the day they were more than happy to give him the highest quality of service and attention as a passenger. But at their invitation, he joined them each evening as an old friend, to yarn about times past.

As I said, to be invited to 'The Pig & Whistle' is a great honour sparingly bestowed. Far from moping miserably in his cabin each evening, Steve Turner was *Ruritania*'s happiest and proudest passenger.

A Life on the Ocean Wave

Though the 'factions' which appear on these pages are based on incidents which occurred on cruise ships, I have other nautical tales to tell that have no need of embellishment.

Quite the most fascinating encounter – and one which led to a couple of articles and an hour-long documentary on BBC Radio Four – happened when I was lecturing on P&O's *Arcadia* in December 2002. I had joined her in Acapulco and remained on board, delivering my lectures, as she made her way down the west coast of South America.

In Lima, Peru, we were berthed for a couple of days and at breakfast, I spotted half a dozen fellows sitting together. I had not seen them before, so they must have come on board the previous evening, having flown to Peru from the UK. All were wearing identical polo shirts, decorated with the logo of the company they worked for. I wondered what had brought them all that way. It had to be something pretty serious. Were they a team of engineers flown out to deal with a technical emergency that was being kept secret from the passengers? Was it, perhaps, a serious medical crisis? My thoughts were turning to bubonic plague when they all rose and left the restaurant.

Over the next few days I watched in astonishment as they went about their highly skilled task: putting up the ship's Christmas decorations.

Their story was a fascinating one. They worked for a company called KD Decoratives. Based in Huddersfield, the firm had the contract to put up Christmas decorations on all P&O cruise ships. Whether this required a team to make a quick trip down to Southampton or a flight to the other side of the globe was, I guess, the luck of the draw.

They told me that the decorations themselves, packed in a couple of cargo containers, had been shipped out to Lima months before, and had been waiting for our ship on the dockside. When you consider the size of P&O's cruising fleet at that time, the logistics behind that worldwide operation must have been mind-boggling.

'I suppose you'll be staying on board to take them down before Twelfth Night,' I said as we sat together one evening.

'Oh, no,' said one of them. 'We're flying back to the UK. The company has contracts to put up Christmas decorations in most of the big shopping malls, so we'll be needed for that.'

And that's exactly what they did. And, in due course, they all flew out again to re-join *Arcadia* and take down the decorations.

Arcadia was the largest ship on which I had ever been invited to talk. I am not partial to big ships.

I delivered my first lecture in the ship's cinema, which, to my delight, was full to overflowing. However, the cruise director had complaints from passengers who could not find a place, so switched me to the show lounge. This was a vast, two-storey space, designed for big presentations, bands and troupes of dancers and lots of razzamatazz. In the centre of that large stage I was a very lonely little figure, with no visual aids or gimmicks to hide behind.

Still, the passengers seemed to appreciate and enjoy my lecture, which was a relief given the conversation I'd had with the cruise director beforehand, asking what would happen if the show lounge proved unsuitable.

'If you don't go down well, I'll move you to a smaller location,' he replied.

'What have you got in mind?'

'How big is your cabin?'

On little ships, lecturers tend to be given other tasks, usually helping with the shore excursions. This help consists of collecting tickets and being sociable, while a local guide as well as a member of the ship's staff shoulder the real responsibilities.

However, when *Ocean Majesty* called at Tallinn on one of her Baltic cruises, a member of the ship's staff could not be spared, so I shepherded my group of 38 into one of the waiting coaches, introduced myself to the local guide, and set off for the organised tour of the city.

All went well at the start. I got my flock on and off the coach with no problems when we stopped for a closer look at sights outside the city boundary. Then we headed into town for the lunch stop, which was combined with a folk dancing performance.

Unfortunately, this was where all the groups met and mingled, and it took a lot of effort to make sure people re-joined their proper groups after the show. But I managed and, following the guide, shepherded my 38 along the streets of Tallinn, pausing now and then to hear what she had to say about this, that or the other aspect of local architecture and history.

Then, to my horror, as we set out on the final leg of the walk towards the coach station, I realised I had only 36 people in the group. I looked very carefully at them and worked out who was missing.

I would have to retrace our steps all the way back to the lunch venue, hoping to find them *en route*. So I told the guide to get everyone on our coach and back to the ship, as planned. I would find my missing couple and bring them to the ship on the shuttle bus.

I searched high and low, but could not find them. I waited until the last possible moment before jumping on the final shuttle bus and getting back on board *Ocean Majesty*. With some trepidation, I reported to the cruise director that I had lost two of my flock.

I expected him to react strongly. I expected a telling-off at least. Even a bawling-out. I expected tantrums and anger.

Instead he shrugged his shoulders. 'Don't worry,' he said. 'I expect they made their own way back on board.'

And we sailed from Tallinn. At the time, I should point out, there was no system of swipe cards, or – more simply – a board beside the gangway on which you hung your cabin key, that would enable the crew to know if anyone remained ashore. I thought the cruise director's attitude somewhat cavalier.

But he was quite right. Later that evening, showered and shaved and dressed for dinner, I went into the bar for my usual 'pre-prandial', and spotted the couple in question.

'Oh,' she said, when I asked what had happened. 'We decided to go shopping and catch the shuttle bus back to the ship. We looked for you to tell you, but you weren't there.'

On reflection, that is probably the closest I have ever come to strangling a fellow human being.

Ocean Majesty was a delightful ship; quite old and past her prime, but massively popular among passengers, who returned to her time and time again. I lectured on her from 2000 until 2002, and recall her Baltic cruises with particular affection – that Tallinn incident apart.

She was, I think, Greek-owned. Her officers were Greek to a man, except for the ship's doctor, who was Bulgarian to a woman.

The crew were Filipino and the cheeriest bunch of rascals it has been my pleasure to encounter, always smiling and pleasant. It took the bar staff hardly any time to memorise passengers' names and the drinks they preferred, the restaurant waiters were attentive and the girls who dealt with wine orders were models of efficiency.

The officers, on the other hand, seemed a little too laid-back for my liking. They were pleasant enough, and efficient when they needed to be, but – as is the case with so many Greek chaps – seemed to think their main mission in life was to bring love and joy into the lives of ladies. The only available ladies being passengers, they set about this task with complete disregard to age or marital status, prowling the decks each evening with wide, vulpine grins.

It's true what they say – 'beware of Greeks baring teeth'.

On each of those Baltic cruises for the three consecutive years that I sailed on the *Maj*, as she was affectionately known, we called at St Petersburg, then being transformed for its upcoming 300th anniversary. No expense was being spared; this was, after all where Vladimir Putin was born, though it was called Leningrad then. The place glistened with lavishly applied gold leaf, and smelled of fresh paint.

Because *Ocean Majesty* was a small ship, she was able to make her way into the heart of the city and moor at the Britannia Quay. It was far handier than the out-of-town cruise terminal where the superliners ended up.

As I leaned against the ship's rail, watching the mooring ropes being secured and taking in the view of a city I had never before visited, I saw a group of Filipinos assembling at the top of a gangway at the rear of the vessel – obviously a shore leave party, free for a few hours. As soon as permission was given, they scampered down the gangway and across the quay. There, they climbed half a dozen steps to reach street level. The street and the quay were divided by a low wall, behind which stood a score or so of ladies. Most, though not all, were young. Most, though not all, were quite presentable. But all were there for a professional purpose.

My fellow passengers and I watched with interest as the lads greeted their new friends, entered into swift negotiations, and either dived with them into waiting taxis, or hurried arm-in-arm around the corner and out of sight.

From our vantage point we exchanged glances. The passengers – overwhelmingly of the older generation – were fairly relaxed about the situation. They were, after all, men and women of the world who had much experience and a 'live and let live' sort of attitude. At least, until they recognised their cabin steward or – more pertinently – their restaurant waiter among the crowd.

One elderly lady summed up the feelings of many: 'I don't really care what the little devil gets up to, as long as he washes his hands thoroughly before he brings my dinner,' she declared firmly.

As we left St Petersburg, the cruise director told me there had been a lot of complaints. Not all the passengers had been as understanding as that old lady. 'I've asked our local agent to do what he can,' he said. 'We've got to shield the passengers from that sort of thing.'

A year passed before the *Maj* once again nosed her way towards the Britannia Quay. Interested to see how the situation had changed, I hurried to the ship's rail. There were no women lining the low wall, but someone had been busy with a pot of paint. From the water's edge, a line of bright yellow footprints made its way across the quay to the steps, up the steps, and diagonally across the road to the doorway of a bar. In that doorway stood two ladies. Their presence, presumably, was confirmation that the rest of the girls were waiting inside.

To drive home the point of the exercise, small representations of male genitalia had been incorporated into the footprints – exactly like those one is shown on the pavements of Pompeii or Ephesus, for, in that respect, time changes nothing.

Down the gangway the shore party ran, to trip happily along the St Petersburg version of the Yellow Brick Road (I must be very careful to spell that correctly), towards the delights that awaited them.

They vanished into the bar, reappearing a few moments later arm-in-arm with the working girls, hailing taxis or hurrying out of sight.

Once again, as we departed, the cruise director joined me at the rail.

'That was a lot better than last time,' I said to the cruise director.

'Yes,' he replied. 'But still not good enough. I've had complaints and have asked the port agent to see what he can do.'

The following year, as we approached the quay, not a single girl was in sight. The yellow footprints were still there, but faded almost to oblivion. However, on the quay was a bus – not a huge tour bus, not a tiny minibus, but something about half way between the two. It had a large, white, vinyl banner tied to one side. In big blue letters was a slogan in the Cyrillic alphabet with, below it, an English translation.

It informed the world in general – and *Ocean Majesty*'s passengers in particular – that the bus was from the Port of St Petersburg's Club for Sailors. If anyone asked, we had been briefed to explain that the port authority, in conjunction with the cruise companies, had set up a club where crews could relax and enjoy themselves in a healthy environment. The bus was their free transport to its chaste delights.

For all I know, they might well have set up such a club. But what I do know for certain is that the lads scampered very happily down the gangway and on to the bus, grinning broadly as it drove off and around the corner.

What went on out of sight was, of course, out of mind.

But as a footnote, I should add that on the second of our trips (the Yellow Brick Road year) I joined a few crew members – two of the girl dancers, the assistant cruise director and a couple of others – and crossed the road to that bar. It was lively and loud, with crew and locals mixing quite happily. Most of the chaps were drinking their Heinekens straight from the bottle, so I felt a little self-conscious as I sat at the bar with mine in a glass, watching the general merriment.

A couple of stools away sat a very beautiful young lady. She smiled when I sat down and, after a moment or two, asked if I was from 'the pretty little ship'. I said I was.

'You travel with your wife?'

I told her I travelled alone, but was not a passenger. I was giving talks on the pretty little ship.

She slipped from her stool and stood next to me.

'You are different from the others,' she said.

I looked at those others, cavorting around the pool table, drinking beer from bottles and generally larking around.

'Yes,' I replied. 'I am much older than they are.'

She laid a tender hand on my thigh, and looked deep into my eyes. 'That need not be a problem,' she declared.

I replied that I was immensely flattered by her attention, but would, regretfully, have to decline.

'Then perhaps you will buy me a drink?'

I agreed, thinking I was about to be fleeced by the old 'fake champagne' routine, but to my surprise she merely asked for an orange juice.

That evening, I described the encounter to a group of officers, whose number included the Bulgarian doctor.

'She would be drinking orange juice because she could not be drinking alcohol,' she said, somewhat tersely. 'When you are taking drugs for certain medical problems, you are forbidden alcohol.'

I thought it best not to ask what the 'medical problems' might be.

White Man's Silver Bird

Returning to the subject of air travel, I must first tell you a story which I am assured is true, though I wasn't there when it happened.

As they waited for their plane to depart on an internal flight in New Zealand, passengers became aware of a strong smell of petrol. Knowing that aviation fuel does not smell of petrol, they were, at first, puzzled, then alarmed.

A member of the cabin crew was summoned. He, too, smelled the petrol and began checking the overhead lockers to trace the source. After a few moments he identified a large parcel, wrapped in heavy duty plastic and securely bound with wide, grey sticky tape. Holding it aloft, he asked its owner to make himself – or herself – known.

A man sitting nearby acknowledged that the parcel was his cabin baggage.

'What's in it?' asked the steward.

'It's my chainsaw,' the man replied.

'How the devil did you get a chainsaw on to an aircraft?' demanded the astonished steward.

'Well,' responded the passenger, 'when I told the girls at the check-in desk what it was, they looked at the list of all the things you aren't allowed to take on to an aircraft. And as there was no mention of chainsaws, they said it would be all right.'

Such stories make me long for the old days, when I first began to travel professionally. The days when you turned up at London Airport and handed in your luggage, receiving in return a boarding pass and directions to the departure gate. You wandered through the gate, had your boarding pass checked and were invited to walk out to the aircraft and take your seat.

It was a procedure known as 'trickle loading', enabling people to settle into their seats as they arrived. A single announcement just before departure was used to round up the stragglers, and off you went.

There was no hanging around waiting to be told where to assemble for your next session of hanging around. No boarding by seat row numbers. No standing in the aisle while inconsiderate travellers tried to cram large bags into the lockers. No 'hurry up and wait' airport routines.

There were certainly no security checks, no loading your coat or handbag on to a plastic tray and sliding it through an X-ray machine. No taking off of trouser belts or shoes. None of the nonsense that everyone knows is a waste of energy and time, but that everyone fears to criticise aloud.

A few years ago I had to depart from Heathrow's recently opened Terminal Five. I had heard terrible stories of how awful it was, but from the moment I dropped off my bag – shortly after 8.30 a.m. – to sitting down with a drink and a Danish pastry in an airside coffee shop took a little under fifteen minutes. I had, in fact, breezed through.

Less than half an hour later, however, returning from the newsagent where I had exchanged a little coupon for my usual morning newspaper, the scene was a very different one. There were queues and confusion.

I watched as a uniformed minion patted down an elderly passenger. The procedure clearly upset the man, who must have been well into his eighties. It certainly distressed his wife, standing next to him. The fact that he was in a wheelchair merely confirmed my view that airport security is sixty per cent nonsense. And forty per cent stupidity. It also adds strength to the anecdotal evidence that such intrusive security procedures are the reason older travellers are forsaking air travel in droves. Certainly those who plan to take their holidays in Europe are travelling by train instead.

Right: having got that little rant off my chest, let me whisk you back in time. Back, for example, to the summer of 1970 when an American carrier called National Airlines began to fly into the UK from Miami. Florida was beginning to attract British holidaymakers, so National figured it would have a slice of the action.

Back then, experienced air travellers were very few and far between. It was a time when, on summer Saturdays at Luton Airport, you would see the majority of passengers dressed formally for their journeys. The ladies would wear 'going away' outfits, with tailored jackets, tight, hip-hugging skirts, high heels, big hair and hats. Chaps were in crisply starched shirts with freshly-pressed trousers, regimental ties, blazers and day-old haircuts. Travel by air was something that only posh people had done up till then. If you were going to join them, you had to look the part.

But looking the part couldn't make up for the fact that you hadn't a clue what happened once you got to the top of the steps.

Which is why National Airlines took it upon themselves, in their newspaper advertisements, to explain to the uninitiated that everything was included. Once you had paid your fare, you were expected to pay nothing else. In-flight meals were free, as were drinks on their services. Unfortunately, they insisted on having their advertising copy written in Madison Avenue, so their first full-page announcements assured potential British passengers that, if they chose National for their journey to Miami, 'you won't be able to spend a penny.'

✈

In some ways I'm sorry I arrived too late to fly in the Boeing 377 Stratocruiser, a double-decked monster which took almost thirteen hours to cross the Atlantic and carried fewer than 120 passengers. Journalists who had travelled on it used to tell me how wonderful the service was, but they were recalling the years immediately after the war, when everything would have been wonderful.

However, I was lucky enough to fly in Concorde – several times. It is a machine that caused great controversy, and required a lot of creative accounting to get it into the air and keep it there. But I loved it.

We have a family memory of watching old Tarzan movies on television, and of one film in particular whose storyline was that the time had come for 'Boy' to leave the jungle and go to school. Tarzan and Jane were sad to see him go (as I suppose, was Cheetah the Chimp), but after a lot of toing and froing – including an unforgettable scene when an old tribal chief gave sage advice to Boy in a broad American accent – the lad was all set to depart. He stood with Tarzan and Jane beside the jungle airstrip. Then there was a cutaway stock shot of a battered old DC3 flying over treetops. As the camera cut back to the trio, Tarzan placed his hand on the boy's head and declared: 'See, white man's silver bird has come to take Boy away.'

So, to my family, Concorde was 'White Man's Silver Bird'. And we had a summer evening ritual of walking into the garden, glass in hand, to toast her as – at the end of her flight from New York – she swung in a long arc down towards Heathrow.

It was a great shame that vested interests, and dodgy American politicians, did their utmost to keep Concorde out of New York. From time to time I visited the city during the late 1970s, when the controversy raged. Regardless of what the Federal Government thought, the New York Port Authority was determined to resist. Experienced observers of the situation concluded that some or all of its members were being bribed by those who had a commercial interest in keeping Concorde at bay. I would not dream of making such a suggestion, but have to say that their arguments were occasionally weird.

On one occasion it was claimed the supersonic boom would break all the windows in all the skyscrapers – regardless of the fact that, by the time it approached the city, it would be flying subsonic. It was pointed out, by those of us who had a few facts at our fingertips, that Concorde regularly flew from its base at Fairford in Gloucestershire, over Cotswold villages whose churches possess some of the finest medieval stained glass in Europe – which is to say in the world. Not one of those ancient panes suffered so much as a scratch. So why should the modern windows of New York be in danger?

At the height of the row I was making a monthly appearance on the *Jimmy Young Show* on BBC Radio Two. I would be wheeled in to answer listeners' travel enquiries and chat generally about what was happening on the travel and holiday scene. On one occasion, knowing I had returned from New York only a couple of days previously, Jimmy Young asked for my thoughts about the ongoing Concorde row.

'As far as the New York Port Authority is concerned, the problem is that Concorde has a basic design fault,' I said.

'And what is that?' asked my genial host.

'It has a Union Jack on the tail, not the Stars and Stripes.'

Jimmy Young hastily put on a record and, as it played, said: 'Now you've put the cat among the pigeons. The phones will start ringing off their hooks.' They did.

Eventually common sense prevailed and the politicians and pressure groups were vanquished. Concorde made it to New York and New York loved her.

I am the only person I know who spent his own money buying tickets to fly on Concorde. Of course, most of my flights were taken in the course of my work when the financial arrangements were out of my hands. But from time to time I had an opportunity to fly in White Man's Silver Bird in a purely personal capacity – and to take my wife along.

It happened this way. There came a time when Concorde was being chartered by travel companies, one of which was Cunard. The popular deal was to fly Concorde to New York, returning to Southampton on the *QE2* (*Queen Elizabeth 2*), or vice versa.

Because I had particularly close links with Cunard, I would occasionally receive a telephone call asking if Sheila and I might be free to fly to New York on a date in the very near future – for example I'd get a call on a Thursday afternoon in relation to the following Tuesday. That was the kind of timescale I'm talking about. If we were free – and we often were – then we would be invited to occupy a couple of Concorde seats that would otherwise be empty. If I remember correctly, the cost was around £400 – for the two of us.

Of course, I had to pay for a New York hotel room for a night or two, depending on how much time we had to spare. And for our seats back to London on a 747. What with all that, not to mention the shopping, it wasn't the cheapest of short-break holidays. However, Concorde was an insignificant element of its cost.

During my years with the BBC's *Holiday* programme, one of my tasks was to set a competition to coincide with the start of the series, and run in conjunction with *Radio Times*. Because the Christmas and

New Year issue of the magazine sold three times its usual number, the competition was launched in that edition with the aim of persuading people to continue buying it, in order to access further clues and entry forms and what have you. Maintaining that higher circulation was good for the advertising revenue, you see. *Radio Times* financed the competition and our job was to set the questions and organise the prizes. In due course the top prize had to involve Concorde.

One year we decided to shoot a commercial promoting the competition, and this, naturally, required us to film on board a Concorde in flight. To cut a long story relatively short, the only flight we could access in the time frame we had was an Air France plane, flying back to Paris from an air show at Castle Donington.

As the flight climbed up from Castle Donington, we set up the 'piece to camera'. Clutching the obligatory flute of Champagne I gazed earnestly into the camera, saying something like: 'Well, this is a wonderful prize, and the start of a wonderful adventure. Our next stop is New York. After that, the unforgettable experience that is the United States of America.'

At this, the lady in the seat behind me said: 'I don't want to worry you, son. But I think you're on the wrong flight.'

So we had to do a second take.

Encounters Down Under

When I began my travel writing career, Australia and New Zealand were countries to which people emigrated – often paying £10 for the one-way journey by sea, taking advantage of a government-backed 'assisted passage' scheme. The idea that such faraway places could be holiday destinations was simply never considered. The same applied to Canada and the United States of America, though our former colonies 'down under' were the magnet for the majority of ambitious emigrants.

As the child of parents who considered relocating to New Zealand immediately after the Second World War, I've watched with interest as those distant places have increasingly featured in our holiday plans. Having acquired an Australian son-in-law and three Australian grandchildren, I am particularly keen on that wonderful country.

My professional travels have taken me to Western Australia, New South Wales and the Northern Territory. Personal reasons have taken me many times to Queensland.

Memories of Alice Springs are strong, as it featured in an early visit. I was with a BBC film crew and we pitched up not knowing what to expect but determined to get the best out of our few days there. It was a difficult shoot, as our director thought the town was, putting it mildly, unsophisticated. I overheard him, very late one evening and slightly the worse for wear, expressing his opinion to the hotel barman.

'This place,' he declared, 'is the *rs*hole of the world.'

'Don't worry about that, sir,' the barman replied. 'After all, you're just passing through.'

I wondered if this was the barman who featured in an encounter that became a Fleet Street legend. According to the story, a well-known national newspaper hack (some claim it was Nigel Dempster) on a visit to Alice had the temerity to ask for a dry sherry. From that instant the barman, and most of the local population, christened him 'that Pommie pooftah'.

Named after Lady Alice Todd, the town was originally the site of a repeater station for the newly-laid telegraph in whose development her husband, Sir Charles Todd, was much involved. We filmed in the original station building where photographs of those pioneers are displayed. Staring fixedly at the camera were men and women in Victorian clothing more suited to a European winter – stiff collars and ties, serge suits and bowler hats, voluminous heavy skirts, high-necked blouses. How they managed in the heat – and, moreover, managed without the comfort of air conditioning or refrigeration – is something of a miracle. But they did.

Finding the highest vantage point, we shot a 'piece to camera' by yours truly. Then, as the crew busied themselves with taking panoramic shots and recording a few minutes of ambient sound, I got into conversation with an Aboriginal chap who had been watching our activities with some interest.

I did so because I wanted to get to the bottom of a story I had been told many years previously, long before the prospect of going to Australia was on my horizon.

According to the tale, back in 1770 a couple of officers from Captain Cook's *Endeavour* had gone ashore and were trying to communicate with some reasonably friendly locals. As they stood together an animal bounded past. A creature they had never seen before. A creature with long legs and a pouch.

With signs and gestures they asked one of the Aborigines what that creature was.

'Kangaroo,' he replied.

What the officers didn't realise was that, in that fellow's language, 'Kan ga roo' meant 'I don't know'.

Now, with this chap standing before me, I could get to the truth of this tale. I did not know then that there are many Aboriginal clans and many Aboriginal languages, so I ploughed ahead in happy ignorance.

'What does "kangaroo" mean?' I demanded.

He pursed his lips and gazed into the distance. (I should perhaps mention at this point that he had been drinking deeply from what appeared to be a gallon jar of wine.) 'Kangaroo?' he asked.

'Yes, "kangaroo". What does it mean in your language?'

He took a deep swig from his flagon, shrugged his shoulders and said: 'I don't know.'

Years later I was on the Queensland coast north of Cooktown, where, in 1770, Captain Cook beached his ship in order to carry out essential repairs. If the encounter in that story had taken place, it would have been there.

By then, I had learned that two nations, or clans, had lived in that southeast corner of Cape York for tens of thousands of years. They were the Guugu-Yimithirr and the Kuku Yalanji, but of more importance was that I was in the company of Willie Gordon, an elder of the former clan, and a storyteller.

We were some distance north of Cooktown in an area of sandstone escarpments, rainforest and scrub and, walking with Willie Gordon through his ancestral lands, listening to his stories, his interpretation of ancient rock art and his dissertations on the uses of various shrubs and plants, I came to understand something of the philosophy of the oldest people on the planet.

He showed me one plant which, when rubbed between the palms of your hands, turns into a soap. Another from which drinkable water can be obtained. He offered me a handful of tiny lemon ants to eat – very tasty and thirst-quenching they were, too.

And he explained the tragedy of how many of the early settlers died of hunger and thirst when they were surrounded by food and water – if only they had known where to look.

His company on that walkabout was so good that I didn't mind at all his smiling demolition of the 'kangaroo' story.

I'd come to Cooktown by way of the Bloomfield Track, a little under fifty miles of rough and rugged 'road', impassable by anything other than a tough four-wheel drive vehicle.

One aspect of Australia that travel writers can never adequately explain concerns time and space.

With 40,000 years of history, the Aboriginal people are the oldest on the planet – far outstripping, say, the Ancient Egyptians. The Daintree Rainforest, which I visited for a few days before my rough ride along the Bloomfield Track, is, similarly, the oldest in the world. According to the people who know about such things, it is 65 million years older than the Amazon.

As for space – or, more accurately, size – let me illustrate that with a simple example.

The constituency of Mount Isa elects one member to serve in Queensland's Legislative Assembly. At the last count, it had a population of just over 22,000, of whom 19,119 were registered voters.

If that description brings to your mind a vision of a quiet outback town at the heart of a small rural district – rather like Rutland – then you need to know that the constituency of Mount Isa is larger than the whole of Metropolitan France (220,272 square miles, compared to France's 212,935 square miles, since you ask).

Once you can get your head around the age of Australia and its mind-blowing size, you can appreciate the character of the pioneers who explored and colonised it, and the multitude of wonderful characters who live there now. They are, without exception, proud of their country and its heritage. And have every right to that pride.

They also have a certain attitude towards British visitors, neatly encapsulated in an encounter during an early filming trip when I was travelling with another BBC director along the Queensland coast.

We'd collected the hire car and were making for Airlie Beach, where we planned to film, among other things, the Great Barrier Reef. We were clipping along at a fair pace when a policeman leaped into the road ahead of us and flagged us down. He had a radar detector and informed us that we were breaking the speed limit. As far as we could tell we were in the middle of nowhere, but he assured us there was a speed limit and Clem, the director, who was driving, had definitely exceeded it.

As he stood there, checking the driving licence and filling in his ticket, he remarked that we were obviously not locals. So we did our 'innocent British visitors' routine, with Clem explaining that we were with the BBC and in the area to make a film encouraging visitors to this beautiful part of a wonderful country. I added my two-pennyworth of praise, hoping it would soften his heart.

'We need as many visitors as we can get,' he said. 'In fact we had a special campaign to encourage local people to welcome tourists.

Especially those from foreign countries.'

Then, as he handed over the speeding ticket, he grinned and added: 'Unfortunately for you two gentlemen, the campaign ended yesterday.'

Towards the end of that trip, I woke up one morning to find I was wearing a T-shirt which bore a slogan saying Air Whitsunday had flown me to the Great Barrier Reef. As the airline had done nothing of the sort, I asked my colleagues at breakfast how I came to be wearing one of its T-shirts.

'You got it at the dance,' said Chris, the cameraman. 'You swapped it for your own shirt. After the barbecue. At the hotel down the road.'

I could not remember the dance, the barbecue or, for that matter, the hotel down the road. But Chris assured me that I had, indeed, exchanged the shirt I had been wearing for that T-shirt when I was cavorting about on the dance floor. He added that later that morning we would be flying out to the Great Barrier Reef with Air Whitsunday.

The Whitsunday Islands lie off the coast of Queensland, and were named by Captain Cook because that was the day he 'discovered' them. Air Whitsunday had a fleet of flying boats, otherwise known as amphibious aircraft, and we used a couple of them to obtain aerial shots of the reef and the coast.

The experience of taking off and landing on the sea is quite remarkable, especially when one then taxies through the waves and up on to busy beaches, as we did on our return. It had a touch of the James Bond about it.

When people speak of the Golden Age of Flying they are usually referring to that time between the wars when Imperial Airways, the forerunner of BOAC, spanned the globe – or, at any rate, that part of it coloured red – with a fleet of very large 'Empire' flying boats. They carried less than twenty passengers in extreme comfort, landing every evening on a suitable stretch of water so those passengers could spend the night in a hotel before continuing to Africa, India, the Far East and Australia. Archive photographs portray them being served 'high tea' as they relaxed in wicker armchairs, or watching films shown on a small screen by means of a hand-operated projector.

Air Whitsunday provided a hint of what that must have been like, though its Grumman Goose was much tinier than the giants of Imperial. We had no wicker armchairs in which to recline, no silver service, and no chief steward to entertain us with his film projector.

But it was great fun to splash down and walk upon the reef, to fly low over the islands and Shute Harbour on the mainland. To roam around Airlie Beach and to know we were getting some tremendous material for our destination report.

One evening, after a highly successful day, we went into town from our motel on its outskirts because there was a race meeting on at one of the main pubs. Toad racing. Now the Cane Toad is a large and generally unpleasant creature, with enough poison in it to seriously damage an adult and possibly kill a child. Or so the Australians claim.

Introduced into Queensland to control some crop-damaging bug, it totally failed to do so and had been a nuisance ever since. But in Shute Harbour that evening, they were going to be racing and, this being Australia, there was going to be some serious betting.

However, when we arrived at the hotel – for some reason pubs tend to be called hotels in Australia – it was to learn that the racing had been cancelled because of a power cut.

In the main bar, by the light of candles and oil lamps, I sought out our host and asked him why the racing had to be cancelled. After all, I reasoned, the toads had no need of electricity as they hopped and scurried along the course.

'You really don't understand, John,' he replied, pouring me a cold beer and downing the remnants of his own. 'Sure, the toads don't need electricity, but with no proper light, how can we tell which one of the little bastards has won?'

That seemed reasonable enough to me, so we concentrated on our beers and our conversation. After a while I noticed a tall and attractive blonde lady who seemed to be eyeing me up from a table near the door. When I smiled at her, she smiled back. I turned to Clem, the director, and said: 'I know it sounds corny, but though I can't remember seeing her before, there's something familiar about that girl.'

'Yes,' he replied. 'That shirt she's wearing is the one you gave her in exchange for the Air Whitsunday T-shirt she had on, a couple of nights ago.'

I looked at the girl with greater interest, noting that she was quite statuesque.

'Clem,' I asked, 'when we swapped shirts, was she wearing…?'

'No,' said Clem. 'She wasn't.'

'Nothing?'

'Nothing at all?'

I heaved a great, sad, sigh, and Clem promised that one day he would try to tell me what I had missed or, more accurately, what I hadn't missed, but could not remember.

I must remind him to do so.

One day.

The Light Fantastic

A major hazard in a travel writer's life, as I have mentioned before, is the inescapable local 'folkloric' performance. I touched on folk dancing and singing when I wrote about that unforgettable trip to Corfu, and the development of the Costa Smeralda on Sardinia. But I have encountered it all over the globe, and often it hasn't turned out as expected.

In Goa, we stayed in a relatively smart hotel on the outskirts of the capital Panaji (which for some reason, we were told, was pronounced 'Panjim'), and spent our days trotting around filming really good stuff. Most of our fellow guests, however, tended to stick close to the hotel and its private beach, as they were overwhelmingly first-timers to India and terrified of what might be encountered beyond the hotel grounds.

I managed to persuade one young couple to venture out, telling them they could hire a taxi from the rank at the hotel gate for the entire day for less than a pound, and the vehicle would always be on hand to rush them back to the hotel in the event of any problem. When I saw them a couple of days later, they said they absolutely hated everything, and the only good thing about their day in Panaji was that they had found a well-stocked Benetton shop. It takes all sorts. But I digress.

As part of our schedule, we were persuaded that really good material would be obtained if we took the sunset cruise from the harbour. During the course of the cruise there would be folk dancing on deck.

So off we went to the harbour where the boat was moored. We boarded, thinking of the fine sunset shots we would get when out at sea. Not to mention the prospect of sari-clad dancing girls and Indian chaps in those glittery tunics which look so good on camera.

The sun was diving fairly rapidly towards the horizon, but the boat showed no signs of departing. When we enquired, our guide explained that the sunset cruise was so called because it departed at sunset. Not before.

No decent shots of the disappearing sun, then. Still, there was always the dancing.

So it was something of a disappointment that the traditional dancing on board was Portuguese, not Indian. Strike two.

I have a theory that, in the Dark Ages, somebody went around the world teaching everybody the same dances. You can't deny that they follow a pretty standard pattern of skipping around and crossing hands and waving handkerchiefs, and the lads and lasses, more often than not, operate in teams of four. The girls have to pretend to be peasant maidens or shepherdesses or lovelorn villagers, while the chaps strut about being simple fishermen or farmers or sometimes military types. But whatever tale they are trying to tell, it always ends up with a lot of clapping and handkerchief waving and rhythmic stamping of booted feet.

Once, on the island of Minorca, I watched a display of local dances which seemed strangely familiar. 'They remind me of Scottish reels and Strathspeys,' I said to our guide.

'This could be because we learned them from the Scottish regiments who were stationed here when Minorca was part of your British Empire,' she replied.

Though anybody who has holidayed in Spain will probably have encountered Flamenco, the sort of shows you see along the Costas are nothing like the real thing. The tourist version is usually performed by ladies in tight spotty frocks, most of whom are old enough and hefty enough to know better, and anorexic young men who have taken an advanced course in sulking. What I regard as the real thing is encountered in Madrid or Seville, in establishments well away from the tourist circuit, whose clientele are steeped in the tradition of the dances and the music and singing which accompany them.

In Catalonia, however, the dance they perform is called the Sardana. It has unbelievably complicated steps and the dancers form an inward-facing circle, arms round each other's shoulders. It reminded me of the Greek Sirtaki dance, and I said as much to my host. He understood exactly what I meant, and said that many people believe the Sardana was introduced to the Catalans by Phoenician traders, who would have known Greece and its islands very well indeed.

So, you see, my theory about that bloke going round the world long ago teaching everybody the same dance might have a basis in fact.

When it comes to folk dancing, however, we English are not entirely blameless, as we do have Morris dancing. Some people say it is a corruption of 'Moorish' dancing, having been introduced into England by Moorish traders, rather like those Phoenicians in Spain. One summer we trotted down to Sidmouth in Devon to film a report for *Holiday*, deliberately choosing the week when the English Folk Dance and Song Society was having its annual shindig.

Sidmouth is a pretty little place. Like many West Country resorts, its heyday was during the Napoleonic wars, when the gentry could not take their holidays in France, and it has gently coasted along ever since.

On our first day, setting up to film some general shots on the seafront, we were accosted by a rather rude gentleman demanding to know who we were and what we were doing in his town. I think he must have been a simple, straightforward busybody, because the handful of people in Sidmouth who needed to know about us certainly did so, and were extremely helpful.

Robin, our sound man, said we were filming a report about the new main road that was to be routed through the town. At which the old gent turned puce and stormed off.

The pubs in Sidmouth were granted late-night extensions when the folk dancers were in town. This was particularly useful as far as the Morris dancers were concerned. As a callow youth I had thought Morris dancers were all cissies, prancing around with their hankies and bells and little sticks. On the contrary, Morris dancers are, in the main, hefty blokes with serious beards who are partial to a drop of decent ale. In Sidmouth, late at night, they would reel towards you, out of the darkness, on their way from one pub to another. And then another.

This could have been dangerous had they not kept their bells on, so you could hear them coming down the narrow, dark streets, stumbling and jingling. And singing ancient ditties in broad Wurzel.

A bunch of them came into the pub where we were having a well-earned pint or two. Or, to be more accurate, two of them came into the gents' at the pub, where I was having a quiet wee. I looked up to find one on either side of me – towering on either side of me. The beard on my left looked at me and said to the beard on my right, 'Here, I think this is the bloke that's on the telly.'

The beard on my right slowly nodded in agreement.

And I thought to myself: 'Now is not a good time to discuss gender issues.'

We filmed a chap on the promenade who billed himself as 'Fernando, the Fairly Accurate Fire Eater'. He was very good. So was his little dog. The climax of the act came when he did a trick involving the dog. As it was supposed to 'fail' and end with the dog completely incinerated, it caused something of a sensation.

There was a group of intensely serious ladies in shawls and scarves performing 'authentic 19th-century Lancashire clog dances'. We filmed them and afterwards, as they stood fanning themselves and panting a little, I went across to ask which part of Lancashire they came from.

'Oh, no,' said their leader in a cut-glass accent. 'We're actually from Surrey.'

'Oh,' I replied. 'I didn't know there were any cotton mills near Guildford.'

This remark did not go down well, and the Surrey ladies were decidedly frosty from then on. Fortunately, not for long.

That evening, after stowing away the gear in our hotel, we returned to the centre of Sidmouth for another well-earned pint or so and a meal in an extremely lively restaurant. Assorted Morris dancers, Surrey 'mill girls' and other folksy terpsichores made up the bulk of the clientele. As the evening wore on, the decibel level increased and the alcohol flowed freely.

In the small hours of the next morning I woke to find myself sprawled on a bench on the wide road which ran along the seafront. On nearby benches were a selection of Morris dancers and ladies from Surrey who appeared to have collapsed from their evening exertions – but melded together in a most artistic way. On the bench beside me was a comatose fire eater.

No, I shall never forget the time I spent in the delightful resort of Sidmouth.

Though, believe me, I have tried.

The Ghastly Brenda
a 'faction'

We were on *Canberra* when we encountered Group Captain Frobisher and his wife, 'the ghastly Brenda'. It was some time in the mid 1960s when the ship was new. My wife and I did a lot of cruising then, and this trip promised to be a pretty standard whirl around the Mediterranean, sailing from Southampton and calling at half a dozen ports in a couple of weeks before heading back towards the Solent and home.

The advantage of not having to fly was that masses of luggage could be taken. Plenty of 'fairy frocks' for the ladies and lots of misnamed 'casual wear' for a time when cruising was much more formal than today. The disadvantage was that one had to endure the Bay of Biscay in both directions, and the Bay of Biscay has a bad reputation as far as cautious cruisers are concerned.

It was on the journey out, with the Bay a little on the skittish side, that we first spotted the Group Captain and his good lady. She was sprawled out on a deck lounger, swaddled in a tartan blanket and looking like death on a low flame – simmering with fury at being laid low so publicly. He was most attentive, bringing cold towels and hot bouillon, while she snapped and snarled at him.

'Not a nice lady,' remarked Sheila. 'She certainly doesn't deserve him.'

I agreed, certainly as far as first impressions were concerned. From what I could tell, beneath the tartan shroud was a short, fat female, while the face that protruded from it was ill-favoured and crowned by a thatch of clearly dyed hair. Even allowing for the seasickness, she struck me as being a most unpleasant person.

We didn't know them by name at that point, of course, but there is a natural process to the first few days of a cruise, a process of introductions and observations that quickly establishes who's who. I have always found bar stewards particularly useful during those early days, but on this occasion there were a couple of fellow hacks and their spouses, as well as mine, to help with the research.

'His name's Frobisher,' Robert said, when we were sitting in the Crow's Nest bar towards the end of the third day. 'Former RAF Group Captain, apparently.'

'He looks like a Groupie,' mused Arthur, who had done his wartime stint in Bomber Command. 'Yes, he's definitely got the Group Captain style.'

Peter Frobisher was a shade over six feet tall, thin as a whip and with a head of white hair which added dignity to his sixty-odd years. Undeniably handsome, he resembled the film star Stewart Granger. (I know that name will be unfamiliar to a younger generation, but they can look him up on Google.) He dressed impeccably, was unfailingly courteous to fellow passengers and staff alike, and, according to our spouses, was causing a few hearts to flutter among the older ladies on board.

But Mrs Frobisher, having recovered from her tangle with the Bay, never strayed from his side. Her darting little eyes missed nothing, and her nasty little imagination created problems where none existed. If he paused to pass the time of day with a female passenger, she reacted by yanking his arm so that he would continue walking the promenade deck with her. She barged into conversations he started with anyone, almost as if she feared he would be snatched from her. I have rarely seen such a display of insecurity.

She was, above all else, a most unpleasant person. If he was not at her side, her summoning cry of 'Peter' – which was delivered as 'Peeetaaah' – was as piercing as a masonry drill. She also drank, which is ordinarily no problem. But could not hold her drink, which always is.

From the extremely embarrassing incident at the captain's 'Welcome Aboard' cocktail party, when she mistook one of the junior officers for a steward and bawled him out for not bringing the gin she had demanded, to an almost nightly situation in one of the bars – usually the Cricketers' Tavern or the Pop Inn – Brenda Frobisher became The Passenger to Avoid.

For statistical reasons alone there are usually several such people on any cruise ship, though I have learned over the years to be more tolerant of them than I was back then. It is not always their fault that they are bores or boors, but the confines of a ship magnify behaviour that goes unnoticed ashore. A ship is like a small village, with a village's propensity for gossip and knowing a great deal about other people's business. If one cannot behave with that in mind, trouble usually ensues. I regard such unhappy people more in sorrow than in anger, and try to be tolerant. In Brenda Frobisher's case, I had to make an exception.

For me, the final straw came when she roundly insulted a group of ladies in the beauty salon – a group which included my wife and the wives of my two colleagues. She claimed an appointment had been made, when it was clearly not in the book. She bawled out the staff, then rounded on the customers who protested at her rudeness. We could hear the row in the barber's shop next door.

On any ship, such an incident is common knowledge within the hour, usually less. By the time the Gala Evening reception started, the whole ship knew of the row in the beauty salon and why Mrs Frobisher's coiffure looked more of a mess than usual. Everyone sympathised with her husband, saddled with such a harridan. And everybody wondered, as people so often do, what on earth had drawn them together. More to the point, what was keeping them together?

One evening before dinner, our group gathered in our usual corner of the Crow's Nest bar, telling Fleet Street stories and, as is the way with journalists, talking about other trips and other ships. But the conversation inevitably swung round to the Frobishers and the ghastly Brenda's latest misadventure.

That afternoon, laden with purchases from the ship's shop, she had for some reason gone up the aft staircase instead of down and found herself by the children's paddling pool. Instead of simply turning back the way she had come, she had got into an argument with one of the lido attendants and ended up getting splashed by a few boisterous kids. We reasoned that, with luck, they were too young to understand the torrent of abuse she hurled at them. But it was yet another incident to add to the list and once again, we found ourselves speculating on what kept the Frobishers together.

'It has to be money,' said Arthur. 'There's obviously plenty of it as far as they're concerned. I know she looks like a bundle of laundry at the best of times, but the clothes she wears are top quality.'

The wives agreed, knowing far more than we did about designer looks and labels and fashion trends. They had also noticed, perhaps a little enviously, how freely Mrs F spent when ashore, and in the ship's shop.

So we concurred there was money in the Frobisher household and came to the obvious conclusion that the ghastly Brenda had it, that dear old Peter had made the mistake of marrying her for it, and was having to live with the unpleasant consequences.

And there it would have ended, had not the Bay of Biscay claimed Brenda as a victim on the homeward run. Actually, I believe she was nothing like as ill as she imagined, but the ship's doctor convinced her that she needed complete bed rest in *Canberra*'s hospital. By putting her out of circulation, he displayed great common sense and consideration for the welfare of other passengers.

Her incarceration meant that Peter Frobisher was free from her clutches for a couple of days. Free to drink and chat at leisure in the bars or lounges or beside the pool. Free to be interrogated by Robert, Arthur and me – and, with much greater success, by our wives.

It was a bizarre story, and I do not think 'bizarre' is an exaggeration. The Frobishers did, indeed, have money. But it was not hers. It was his, from a business founded by his grandfather and sold for a very considerable amount shortly before he retired from the RAF. With more than enough to live on in considerable comfort for the rest of his life, came retirement, and the opportunity for Peter Frobisher to seek out a childhood sweetheart, recently widowed, and to marry her after a lifetime of bachelorhood.

The ghastly Brenda was, in his words, 'the love of my life', though she had rejected him many years previously and had now clearly married him only because of his wealth. Her absence in the ship's hospital truly upset him, and he was terribly anxious for her return. 'I simply can't manage without her,' he said with an air of desperation. 'My darling Brenda. She has made my life complete after all those lonely years. So vibrant. So lively.' And tears welled up in those piercing blue eyes.

Hard though it was to believe, that elegant and handsome man was besotted with that awful woman.

As we assembled in the luggage hall after disembarking at Southampton, and I heard Brenda's penetrating voice once more summoning 'Peeetaaah', I reflected, not for the first time, that love may well be blind, but it can also be deaf and, sometimes, tragic, too.

A Bed for the Night

The best and the worst of hotels are equally unforgettable – as are just a handful of those in between.

The vast majority – and I have stayed in hundreds – are not at all memorable because they did what was required of them without a fuss. They didn't let me down but, by the same token, they didn't do anything out of the ordinary during the time I occupied one of their rooms.

I once described the multi-storeyed hotels thrown up along the Spanish Costas as 'Benidormitories'. A chum branded similar establishments 'filing cabinets for people'. And such hostelries exist all over the world: hotels which could be anywhere, blandly decorated, blandly furnished; smooth and efficient and giving you absolutely nothing in the way of an 'experience'.

I must not criticise them – indeed, I do not – because they give their guests just what their guests want. A comfortable home away from home, familiar food, an unlimited number of television channels in an unlimited number of languages and complete insulation from the realities of wherever in the world they happen to be.

However, in my view, that is not the object of travelling. So I shall get on with recalling the hotels that stood out from the crowd.

When I first visited the Kaya Hotel in Uçhisar, Turkey, going back at least forty years, maybe more, it was newly opened and had been welcoming guests for barely a year. Then, the Turkish government was encouraging investment in tourism projects by handing out generous grants, and I was told that the local folk had come up with the idea of this hotel in order to qualify for a shedload of much-needed cash. It was their pride and joy.

Once you got past the fact that it was, actually, a really large cave hollowed out of the soft Cappadocian rock, the unique appeal of the Kaya lay in its bathrooms, where over the washbasin were four taps.

For hot and cold water. And red and white wine.

The locals had contracted the hotel rooms to Club Méditerranée, on whose holidays the wine is always complimentary. A bottling plant was fortuitously located close by, so pipes were laid from it to the hotel and into all the bathrooms.

Such an amenity might upset those who make a big fuss about wine and fret over vintages and suchlike. But the imaginative plumbing system did not seem an affront to anybody staying at the Kaya. I was told that some French clients had a little moan at the outset, but their complaints were sorted out by the use of stainless steel rather than copper pipes.

I am told the facility no longer exists, which is a pity.

When it comes to the worst hotel, the wooden spoon has to be presented to the Hotel HB on Heimaey, the largest of the Vestmannaeyjr – or Westman Islands – located off the south coast of Iceland.

I pitched up in that merry spot in 1965, in the company of a pleasant chap who was on the feature writing staff of *The Daily Telegraph*. He may well have been one of their editors, but time has dimmed the details, as time tends to do. By chance, our visit coincided with an international fishing competition, and for reasons which were not clear, this chap and I were mistaken for the British team.

Now I'm pretty sure there must be a worthy organisation in the UK which regulates sea angling, and just as sure they would have sent along a team had they been able to do so, presuming the Icelandic organisers had asked them. But as nobody else vaguely fitting the description had turned up, we were going to have to represent our country, come what may.

The Hotel HB was, of course, full of damp, smelly fishermen who spent all their time drinking instead of eating and sleeping, but as the food was ghastly and the bedrooms awful, I think they may have known what they were doing.

My own room was the size of an ambitious broom cupboard, just big enough for a single bed and a tiny chest of drawers. The wardrobe was a length of broom handle jammed into an alcove – I only knew it was the wardrobe because there was a single wire coat hanger on the broom handle. A broken wire coat hanger.

The room also contained a small washbasin with two taps. One tap had a blue dot on it, the other a red dot. This could have been because the hotel wished to appeal to an international clientele and feared there might be a language barrier, as the Icelandic words for 'hot' and 'cold' are little known outside Iceland.

On that first morning I ran the red tap. The water was, as I half-expected, quite cold. I shaved painfully, cutting myself in the process.

Then I turned on the blue tap in order to clean my teeth. And scalded my gums.

Icelandic plumbers are either colour blind, or have a warped sense of humour.

We set out early in the company of a taciturn local who spoke no English – and very little Icelandic, come to that. He steered our small craft – no more than a rowing boat with an outboard engine – to the appointed spot, killed the engine and lay back, smoking his pipe and stroking his beard, while we got on with the fishing. We dropped long lines from our borrowed rods, hauling up a lot of coalfish. But the stationary boat pitched and tossed and we were comprehensively sick for quite a while before Captain Birdseye deigned to restart the engine and take us home.

Back at the hotel we told the organisers that Great Britain would, regretfully, have to withdraw from the contest. I think the offence this caused may have led to the Cod Wars, but cannot be sure. During that trip, however, as a result of an extremely merry evening spent in the company, among others, of the mayor and the chief of police, the chap from the *Telegraph* and I sailed with them out to the bubbling island of Surtsey.

Less than a couple of years previously – in November 1963 – volcanic activity had created Surtsey. By the time of our visit, the bubbling and popping and erupting had pretty much died away, but the island was still a touch on the shuddery side, and there were places where you'd burn your backside if you sat down on a handy rock.

In his cups, the mayor had somewhat foolishly confessed that he had never set foot on Surtsey, as it was out of bounds to all but a handful of scientists who lived in a little hut on its edge, doing scientific stuff as nature reclaimed the smoking, barren, landscape. Birds dropped seeds from other islands that had lodged in their feet, and pooed and did all sorts of other things, which was causing tiny green shoots to grow.

We all urged him to assert his mayoral authority and visit the place. We, of course, would go with him. And so we did.

On the approach of our boat, the scientists ran to the shoreline waving and shouting at us to stay away. But the mayor said he had representatives of the British scientific press with him. After a spot of mutual Icelandic yelling, the boffins reluctantly agreed we could come ashore. They tailed us closely and wouldn't let us touch anything, or pick up sea-smoothed driftwood from the beach. However, when they weren't looking, I snaffled a couple of large green glass balls, one of which had some old string woven round it. I was told they were fishing net floats. They are now hanging in my garden shed.

So, it was with mixed feelings I learned that the 1973 eruption of the Eldfell volcano had deposited several thousand tons of ash on Heimaey. I was, of course, sad for the 4,000 or so inhabitants. But I wasn't sorry to see the back of the Hotel HB.

On a subsequent visit to Iceland I stayed, with a television crew, in a hotel near Lake Mývatn. It was in a staggeringly beautiful location, miles from anywhere. It was also, unfortunately, a temperance establishment. The plaintive cries of my colleagues haunt me to this day.

To get from my worst hotel to the most magnificent I ever encountered requires us to travel from one island to another.

From Heimaey to Hawaii.

What used to be called the Hyatt Regency at Waikoloa is now the Hilton Waikoloa Village and, I'm told, just as magnificent as it was when I encountered it in its former guise and glory back in 1990.

Then, it had been open less than two years. Located on an extensive lava flow, it spread over 35,000 acres with hotel rooms, apartment blocks, restaurants, shops and all the trimmings. There was a golf course and, when you consider that its manicured greens were also located on the lava, you can imagine what a feat it was to keep it in championship condition, let alone create it in the first place.

You had to take a tram or a motor boat from the reception desk to the accommodation blocks. I chose the motor boat, as it was 'skippered' by a comely maiden in a tight T-shirt and very short shorts. As it actually ran on rails under the water, she didn't have much to do, except adopt a graceful pose and be stared at.

There was several million pounds' worth of art hanging on the walls of its corridors, displayed tastefully in huge glass cases and simply standing around. 'The world's largest collection of hotel art,' the brochure claimed. I would not argue. There were also carriages drawn by Clydesdale horses, for what purpose I never discovered.

The main swimming pool – of course, there was more than one – was so big I refused to venture into it without checking the shipping forecast.

I've stayed in many a grand establishment, before and since, but have to say the Hyatt Regency Waikoloa was head and shoulders above all of them.

However, the Hotel of the Virgin, at a place called Cuntis in Galicia, Spain will always remain in my memory for quite different reasons.

We were in that region one summer, filming for *Holiday* and travelling from one location to another. During the course of a week we stayed in three hotels of which the last, for two nights, was the Hotel of the Virgin.

When I received the filming schedule in advance of the trip, I wondered, in passing, how we had managed to get seven rooms in a four-star hotel at the height of the holiday season, but put it down to luck. I should have known better.

The filming went well, the other hotels were very reasonable, and we were in high spirits when we drove to Cuntis for those last two nights before returning to London. Our high spirits were not to last.

The hotel looked not unlike a fortress, with high, crenellated walls and a forbidding exterior. But that wasn't the worst of it. Once inside, you became aware of the all-pervading smell of rotten eggs.

What we had not known was that the hotel was a thermal establishment, built, literally, on top of a natural hot spring, and the vast majority – bulk would be an appropriate description – of its guests were there to be treated for a variety of exotic ailments. Skin conditions, in the main.

These guests wandered the corridors and grounds in voluminous white towelling robes. They wore them all day, around the swimming pool and in the restaurant, as they waited for their next appointment in the treatment rooms.

Chris, Robin and I decided to inspect these facilities for ourselves. They were, of course, deep in the bowels of the hotel, where our footsteps echoed from white tiled walls and the rotten-egg smell got stronger and stronger.

Mucky water seemed to be at the heart of the treatments, as guests – or should that be patients – were dipped into baths or hosed down by unsmiling attendants. The various treatment rooms had lots of plumbing. Thick pipes, little red wheels and highly-polished brass valves. I was reminded of the controls of the submarine *Nautilus* in the film version of *Twenty Thousand Leagues Under the Sea*. It was very Victorian. And a tiny bit scary.

We learned that the church sent a lot of its people to this hotel. Wrapped in most of those towelling robes were scrofulous priests and nuns.

The oddest thing, however, was that the unsmiling chaps who wielded the hoses down in the depths sometimes doubled up as waiters. The style of their waiting left a lot to be desired, and I felt they should really stick to the hosing and the dipping.

Just for the fun of it, I paused from writing this to look up the Hotel La Virgen Termas on a web site, and read the comments posted by guests. Most of them were in Spanish, but from what I could gather the dear old place is still going strong – and still smelling of rotten eggs.

Mrs Thompson

I have mostly good memories of the USA. Having travelled there more times than I can recall, I have seen it change, ever so gradually, mainly for the better. For one thing, it is now possible to get a decent pint of beer instead of the fortified lemonade that dominated the scene all those years ago. And for another, most Americans now really do know what is going on in the wider world.

Remember, it was fifty years ago when I first encountered the USA. 'The past is a foreign country', wrote L P Hartley. As far as America is concerned, it is another planet.

Back in those early days, the average American knew little about the wider world, and cared even less. And it was easy to understand why this was so. All you had to do was watch local television news, dominated as it was by stories from whichever state you happened to be in, with an occasional nod in the direction of Washington and the national scene. The rest of the world featured only as an afterthought, and then very rarely. Nothing less than the assassination of the Pope could have got Italy on to the news.

'Gee, you're from England.' the waitress would remark, on hearing the accent. 'I sure love your queen.'

Surprised that she should even know Elizabeth Regina existed, I never could get used to being given ownership of her, or, indeed, of everything else in England. The most memorable example being when a fellow who had actually visited Britain (by which he meant

London) said he and his wife had really been impressed by 'your crown jewels'.

They're mine? If only somebody had told me.

The USA is very different now, mainly because far more young Americans travel the world than their parents did, and also in great part because they are far more exposed to foreign (mainly English) programmes on television. As a result, many Americans think we live in Downton Abbey or Ripper Street, with nothing in between. But, even if Midsomer Murders leads them also to believe we spend all our time bumping each other off, at least they get to see our countryside, which can't be bad.

In passing, the American Public Broadcasting Service, which is advertising-free and modelled on the BBC, made the bold decision several years ago to show *Eastenders*. For me the best part was the chap who came on the screen before each episode to give viewers a rundown on rhyming slang and other linguistic eccentricities encountered in Albert Square. Needless to say, the experiment was short-lived.

But I wanted to tell you here and now about Mrs Thompson, who has a prominent place in the story of my very first visit to the USA.

It was in 1964 or 1965, when I was writing travel articles for the Kemsley group of regional newspapers. Three of these were published in Newcastle upon Tyne: the morning *Journal*, the *Evening Chronicle* and the *Sunday Sun*.

An enterprising travel firm in that city came up with the idea of organising a trip to America exclusively for readers of those papers. I was contacted by the *Journal*'s editor once the ball was rolling, and asked if I would accompany the group and write about the trip for his and our other publications. I agreed instantly, as I had never been to the USA; this was a great opportunity to broaden my horizons.

As things worked out, not quite enough Newcastle readers took up the offer, so the group was reinforced by readers of our two papers in Aberdeen.

About a week before the departure date, an excited BOAC public relations officer rang me to say that, for the first time in its history, the airline was going to change the departure time of its scheduled flight to New York at the request of the Newcastle travel firm because – also for the first time in its history – one of its flights had been completely filled by a single group.

It was a strange experience, boarding an empty 707 at London Airport for the flight to Prestwick, where the Newcastle and Aberdeen passengers would be boarding. I have never since had an entire plane to myself. The in-flight service was brilliant!

Apart from me and 180 or so readers, a photographer from the Newcastle *Evening Chronicle* and the organiser of the trip were on the plane when we headed over the Atlantic to New York. I think the travel chap was called Andrew.

The trans-Atlantic flight was uneventful – apart from the fact that BOAC had cleverly arranged for the cabin crew to be Geordies, so it was rather like one long party. It was when we had all passed through Customs and Immigration and been taken by coaches to our Manhattan hotel that the first tiny blip appeared on the horizon.

I was invited to join Andrew and a bunch of American chaps in his hotel room. When I got there, the beers had been opened and discussions were well under way.

The logistics of the trip meant splitting the group into five coaches for an extensive tour of the northeastern states that was to begin the following morning. The chap from the coach company was there to report that he had the coaches and five drivers all set for the morrow.

However, he had only four tour guides, all of whom were in Andrew's hotel room, doing severe damage to his minibar.

'You'll have to be the tour guide on the fifth coach,' Andrew told me.

'How the devil can I be any sort of guide,' I retorted. 'This is the first time I've set foot in America.'

The chap from the coach company dismissed this with a wave of his hand. It would not be a problem, he explained, because each evening I would get together with the other four guides and they would brief me about the following day's schedule – the route we'd be taking, the rest stops, the lunch stop, the places we'd pass, the sights we would see, along with some useful historical and other information.

If I paid attention, made lots of notes, and delivered all that information with an air of confidence, none of my charges would know that it was a case of the blind leading the blind.

And that is precisely what I did for the whole of the ten-day trip.

Some of my friends who know this story reckon it formed the basis for my entire career – confidently bluffing the world into believing that I know things, when in fact I don't. I think this is a wicked calumny, but then I'm biased.

We headed from New York to Philadelphia, we went to Washington DC, over the border to Montreal, and finished up in Boston, from where we flew back to Prestwick. These cities were not the entire itinerary, but I can't for the life of me recall the other, smaller places where we stopped.

There were what you might call 'incidents' along the way. Keen to impress its British guests, one hotel laid on a Polynesian evening, with hula dancers and fire eaters and a suitable spread of exotic food. It was an abject failure, as the group preferred food they could recognise. I felt sorry for the hotel staff who had gone to so much trouble, not to mention the chef and his team, but I guess that's show business.

In Washington I had been instructed to advise my group to go to the Smithsonian Institute's cafeteria for lunch. Lunches weren't included in the deal, as it was thought people would prefer to do their own thing, and quite a lot were happy with a sandwich on a park bench. However, a tour of the Smithsonian had been part of our Washington itinerary, and as it finished at lunch time, the cafeteria was an obvious choice.

I did not, of course, mention that it provided the coach drivers and guides with a free meal – as did all of the recommended restaurants.

So there I was, sitting with the other guides and drivers at our table in the corner when I looked up to see one of my passengers standing over me. He was holding a tray, and had a puzzled look on his face.

He explained that, waiting at the counter, he had scanned the menu, and asked for pie and chips. He showed me, with a touch of annoyance, what was on his tray. Instead of the hot meat pie and chips he was expecting, he had been given a slice of apple tart and a packet of crisps.

Whoever described us and the USA as 'two nations divided by a single language' was spot on.

In Montreal, one of the elderly passengers had a mild heart attack. Fortunately it happened in his bedroom and his wife phoned reception and got the hotel doctor to him in very short order. It did not look to be serious but, to be on the safe side, Andrew arranged for the couple to be flown home that evening. We were spending a couple of nights in Montreal, so Andrew and I were able to accompany the pair of them to the airport and see them safely on their flight. He was full of positive, comforting, words, assuring them that they would be met by an ambulance and trained medics on arrival. And, of course, the cabin crew would keep a close eye on them throughout the journey.

After their flight had departed we retired to an airport bar for a steadying draught. Then another. Then we made our way back to the hotel bar and sat quietly nursing a third. All the while Andrew kept glancing at his watch.

After a while, and two more drinks, he gave a sigh of relief, and smiled.

'They've reached the point of no return,' he said.

I had no idea what he meant, but he explained that, according to his calculations, the flight had passed the half-way mark, so if an emergency arose it would continue to the UK and not return to Montreal. The problem was now out of our hands.

However, the most memorable incident came towards the end of the trip, in Boston, where we were spending two nights before flying home.

Shortly after our arrival, an elderly Scottish lady, travelling alone, buttonholed Andrew with a special request. I was with him at the time, so got her story from the outset, and was subsequently involved in the arrangements that had to be made. Like many British people, Mrs Thompson was a tremendous fan of President Kennedy, who had been so cruelly assassinated in the November of 1963. She had read all about him and his family and their glamorous lifestyle, and thought he was a wonderful fellow. Well, we all did then, I suppose.

She knew that Boston was in Massachusetts. And that so was Hyannis Port, where the Kennedy family had spent so much time. It was her dearest wish to go to Hyannis Port.

Andrew pointed out that this would be extremely difficult to arrange, as we were returning to the UK the following evening.

He could see no way of laying on a special trip for her that would get her back in time for the return flight.

'That doesn't matter,' replied Mrs Thompson – who was, I should mention, around eighty years old. 'If you can change my ticket I'll fly back later.'

There was no dissuading her. In vain the tour guides pointed out that, Labor Day having passed, just about everything in and around Hyannis would be closed for the winter. Mrs Thompson was determined. And convinced it could all be arranged.

So it was. Andrew made a lot of telephone calls, as did the American chaps. And the following morning – when the rest of the group were enjoying a final day 'at leisure' to do some independent sightseeing and shopping – Andrew and I took Mrs Thompson to the Greyhound bus station.

The appropriate ticket was purchased and we walked with her to the door of the bus. We told her where she should get off (having briefed the driver to make sure she did) and that someone would be waiting with her name on a board and a car to take her on to Hyannis Port.

There, accommodation for four nights had been arranged, and the hotel staff would tell her about the local sights and amenities she might like to visit. The deputy manager had been instructed, over the telephone by one of our American chums, to put her on the bus for the return trip to Boston where another person with another name board would make sure she got to the airport in time for her flight.

We had planned the whole thing like a military operation. Every single step of the way, every single aspect of the trip, was covered. We felt tremendously responsible for dear old Mrs Thompson who, if truth be told, really had no idea of what she was doing. We had tried to leave nothing to chance.

Nevertheless, I was worried for her. As the last of the passengers boarded the bus, and she turned to join them, I gave her my business card.

'I want you to promise to ring me when you get home,' I said. 'I shall worry about you until I hear you are back safe and sound. And I've put my home phone number on the back, so you can contact me any time.'

She took my card, telling me not to make such a fuss. And promised faithfully that she would, indeed, make that call.

All this was, as I said, more than fifty years ago.

I'm still waiting to hear from her.

Gently Down the Stream

I know we were in Switzerland, and I think it might have been 1995 or 1996 – a long time ago, I admit, but, though I may not yet have qualified for a free television licence, I was well within free bus-pass territory. We were making a destination report for the television travel show *Wish You Were Here…?* I'm not exactly sure which particular bit of Switzerland we were in, but I seem to recall going on a train that went up *inside* a mountain, the Jungfraujoch.

At the end of the line we got off the train – still inside the mountain – and entered something called the Ice Palace, located inside a glacier. The first thing I saw was a trio of Japanese ladies in traditional kimonos having their picture taken, giggling and shivering at the same time as they stood before a larger-than-life-size statue of Sherlock Holmes, carved in ice.

The Mikado meets *The Hound of the Baskervilles*. And very surreal. But I digress.

It began much the same as most working trips began. A brief as to the kind of story we were looking for, some research before departure and then a flight out to start gathering relevant images and sound, a few interviews if necessary and two or three pithy pieces to camera by yours truly.

It was the type of story I had produced many times. A visit to a region better known for its winter attractions to see what it offered in the summer – a season when cable cars whisked visitors up to walking rather than skiing terrain: when the older and less agile wandered through flower-strewn meadows, tackling the gentlest of slopes on their way to a nice cream tea in a picturesque village.

We'd lay melodies from *The Sound of Music* over most of the long shots (I know it's not the correct country, but the sentiment's the same), and make sure Harry, the sound recordist, recorded plenty of cowbells. Should we encounter any happy ramblers in the right age bracket I would infiltrate their ranks and maybe even interview some of them.

Tom (cameraman) and Dick (assistant cameraman) would be more than happy, as the scenery would be spectacular and they could indulge in the long, slow panning shots that cameramen love – and which, incidentally, were a boon to those of us who wrote our own commentaries (and not everybody did, but that's another story).

As I say, it was all straightforward and predictable. Or so I thought.

For reasons which escape me to this day, Doug (film director) decided to broaden the scope of the report to include sequences that would appeal to our younger and more active viewers. I wasn't especially happy about this, as the things he had in mind could cause harm to an old duffer like me. Mountain biking, for example.

We compromised on the mountain biking. The liaison lady from the local tourist office rounded up some suitable lads and lasses. Tom and Dick filmed them travelling at high speed downhill, on rough tracks through trees. And I added a few words, off screen, along the lines of 'and for those who want something a little livelier, this should provide the thrills…'

There was talk of rock climbing, too. Having brought no equipment with me (who would?) I managed to wheedle my way out of that. We took some suitable pictures, I said something – again, off screen – about having a head for heights, and that was that.

Now I don't want you to think I am not up for anything adventurous or even hazardous. From my earliest days as a travel writer and reporter, I have been prepared to give things a go, especially during the thirty years of my television travel career.

In those long-ago days before the camera drone was invented, the only way to get aerial shots was to hire a helicopter. And the first thing we did with it was take the door off so the cameraman could work unimpeded. Most of the helicopters I have flown in have been doorless. There was no other way to do it, though it carried an element of risk.

Similarly, when required to do so, I ran with the bulls at Pamplona – every morning for a week – though I was much younger then, and I have to admit that alcohol played its part. So I am no coward. However, with age comes caution.

After four days in Switzerland, and just when I thought I was going to complete this assignment in one piece, Doug came up with his masterstroke.

'Whitewater rafting,' he said one evening, towards the end of a very decent and quite well-lubricated dinner. 'I hear you can go whitewater rafting in this area.'

The liaison lady, also reasonably well-lubricated, said it would be no problem to get that organised for us. Which, next morning, she proceeded to do.

Thus it came to pass that we assembled in the lobby of our hotel to meet half a dozen young locals who were to take us on our little adventure. They were impressive, being all very tall and unbelievably fit. In winter they were ski instructors, and during the rest of the year switched to being mountaineers. If I had to go whitewater rafting with anyone, these lads were ideal companions. However, I hoped it wouldn't come to that, as I had a little plan.

We squeezed into wetsuits, then squeezed into a couple of long-wheelbase Land Rovers to drive to our starting point. *En route* we dropped off cameraman Tom at a high point overlooking the river, from which he could film us passing. Assistant Dick, with a smaller, waterproof, camera, would join Doug and me in the large rubber inflatable boat, moored and waiting for us a few miles upstream.

When we got there, Harry, declaring firmly that 'You won't need location sound for this,' remained in the Land Rover.

As we clambered from bank to boat, I mentioned that I couldn't swim. Would this be problem?

Instead of saying that it would, and I would have to stay behind, one of the lads replied that if the boat capsized we should lie back on the water and let the current take us feet first.

Swimming was not an option in such fast-flowing water. (He didn't mention, until long afterwards, that swimming wouldn't help, as we would be instantly dashed to our deaths against the rocks.)

So my plan had come to nought. The river was extremely fast and foamy. I don't know if 'foamy' is a proper word, but that's what it was. Extremely foamy. And bubbly and, when it wasn't foamy and bubbly, clear and green. And dangerous.

It rushed and roared beyond control between steep banks, as the melting snows of spring swelled its course. It tumbled and twisted past great smooth rocks, black and brown and all too obviously lethal. But there was no turning back as we climbed into the boat.

We settled ourselves in. And cast off.

Within seconds the boat was travelling at high speed between the rocks, bouncing and bobbing and taking us where it willed, despite the efforts of the lads to steer it away from the worst of the dangers.

I clung to the ropes attached to the rounded sides of our craft, loudly blaspheming and praying in equal measure.

After what seemed like an hour – in reality about fifteen minutes – the river calmed down and we drifted to the shore where the Land Rovers, having raced down the road, were waiting for us.

On the bank, trembling and dripping, I heard Dick say his waterproof camera had proved to be nothing of the sort, so there would be hardly anything worth using from him. Tom chimed in with the comment that, having filmed us passing, he had, on the way down, spotted an even better vantage point from which he could get some sensational shots to make up for the lack of footage from Dick. However, this required us to do the whole thing again.

And we did. Don't ask. I don't want to think about it.

Eventually we made it back to our hotel, stripped off our wetsuits and joined the lads in the bar for restorative brandies.

'You did very well, for a man of your years,' one of them said, towering over me and waving his brandy glass in an expansive fashion. I was about to make an appropriately barbed response when I realised I was not merely old enough to be his father, but pretty close to being the same age as his grandfather.

So I said: 'Well, you obviously knew what you were doing, so I felt quite confident. Incidentally, how many times have you made that run?'

'Including the two runs today?' he asked.

'Including the two runs today,' I replied.

'Three times.'

'*Three times!*' I stared in disbelief. '*Only three bloody times!*'

And then the truth was reluctantly revealed. The liaison lady hadn't wanted to let us down, so she had asked her chums to obtain a rubber boat, find a stretch of fast river and take us down it.

Only the previous day they had tried out that particular stretch of that particular river and, having somehow survived, decided it would do. They didn't usually do whitewater rafting, being too busy being ski instructors or climbing mountains, but hadn't wanted to disappoint us.

People used to tell me, 'Honestly, what a job. Life's one long holiday for you.'

Yeah. Right.

Miss Priestley's
Shipboard Secret
a 'faction'

When it comes to keeping secrets, as I have mentioned before, a cruise ship is much like a small village, with many sharp eyes and inquisitive minds.

Unless you are very careful, your little foibles and – dare I say? – your indiscretions or peccadilloes are very soon common knowledge.

But because everyone on board the liner *Bombay* sympathised with Jennifer Priestley, her late night activities were kept secret from the maiden aunt with whom she was travelling.

'A conspiracy of silence,' my chum Peter called it. As a travel writer, Peter was partial to a cliché, but though not original the phrase was certainly accurate.

Jennifer was in her late twenties. Her aunt, Edith Priestley, was a year or so past sixty. They had embarked, as we all had, at Southampton for a two-week voyage around the Mediterranean, and for the first few days did nothing to draw attention to themselves.

They remained together throughout the day, with Jennifer dutifully attending to her aunt's needs – securing deck loungers, settling her aunt into them, bringing drinks from the bar and books from the library and generally ensuring the old girl's well-being. Aunt Edith was clearly used to this kind of treatment, and Jennifer clearly used to providing it.

I felt sorry for Jennifer. She seemed to be a dowdy young woman with a face devoid of make-up, hair scraped back, and a tendency towards shapeless, loose-fitting tops and long baggy skirts or trousers. The skirts were, for the most part, sludge-coloured tweeds. Her aunt, by contrast, wore stylish leisure wear, fashionable and clearly expensive evening attire, and had well-groomed hair and carefully applied make-up.

'A striking woman,' someone said one morning as I stood at the Lido Bar, watching Edith Priestley settling herself down for a morning of reading and sunbathing.

I turned to see Roland Bradshaw, a fellow member of the press group on board. It was a working trip for half a dozen travel writers, but in those years, around the 1960s and early 1970s, the work was far from onerous.

Bradshaw – known to us all as 'Puffer' because of his ever-present pipe and his surname, and the fact that he was an expert on train travel – was something of a legend on the travel writing scene. He was a father figure, too, dispensing advice to youngsters like me from the experience of more than forty years 'on the road'. His natural as well as his professional curiosity had required him to take the trouble to talk to the Priestleys and get the facts from Aunt Edith.

'Jennifer's father was Edith's brother. He and his wife were killed in a road accident about ten years ago. In Africa. Kenya, I think,' Bradshaw explained in his usual succinct fashion. 'The old girl took her in, of course. They live in Somerset and always cruise together. Got a couple of single cabins on 'C' deck. Want to know any more?'

I said I didn't. And bought him a beer.

After dinner on the fourth day Jennifer Priestley appeared in the cocktail bar. This in itself was unusual because on previous evenings she and her aunt had retired to their cabins immediately after dinner – or, rather, after coffees and a modest nightcap in one of the bars. But what was more unusual was her appearance.

The scraped back hair was down, long and gleaming. Her face glowed with colour and the evening dress into which she had changed fitted snugly, revealing long, shapely legs and a figure that could stop traffic.

Within minutes she was the centre of attention, especially as far as the young officers were concerned. She laughed and flirted and positively sparkled. She danced energetically and well, and was clearly capable of dealing with a martini or three.

'What a transformation,' I said to Bradshaw, but he had drained his glass and was preparing to leave.

'We're at Villefranche tomorrow morning,' he said. 'I'm on one of the early shore excursions. I trust you'll enjoy the cabaret.' And with a cursory nod in Jennifer's direction, he left the bar.

So a pattern was established. Every evening, having presumably ensured that her aunt was sleeping, a transformed Jennifer would appear and proceed to party into the small hours. Next day, back in dutiful and dowdy mode, she was at Aunt Edith's side. And every single passenger kept Jennifer's secret. Not a word out of place, not a hint dropped to Edith about her niece's late night antics. It was quite amazing, a 'conspiracy of silence' indeed.

As we made our way around the Mediterranean and back towards the Straits of Gibraltar and home, the Priestleys became far more sociable and relaxed than they had been at the start of the voyage.

I could understand this as far as young Jennifer was concerned, for I presumed her opportunities for partying at home were somewhat limited. I also wondered if she looked after Aunt Edith full time, or if she perhaps had a job. Either way, life in Somerset would be nothing like life at sea.

'I think the Priestleys have found the cruise relaxing,' I observed to Bradshaw on the final afternoon. 'Obviously her evenings off the leash have done Jennifer a world of good.'

Bradshaw knocked out his pipe, grunted a comment, and toddled off to change for a pre-dinner drinks party.

I didn't see him again until we were on the train heading to Waterloo. He joined me as we pulled out of Southampton and within a few minutes we were discussing the Priestleys.

Once again, I expressed amazement that Jennifer's late night activities had been kept from her aunt – 'especially when you consider how hard it is to keep anything secret on a cruise ship...'

To my surprise, Bradshaw smiled as he filled and lit his pipe. Then he murmured 'Why do you assume that Edith *didn't* know about Jennifer's behaviour?'

Before I could react he hit me with a second question. 'And why do you assume that Jennifer was the *only* Priestley with a shipboard secret?'

By the time we reached Waterloo, I had prised the story from him.

While Jennifer was the centre of attention each evening, Aunt Edith was enjoying the company of a gentleman suitor – in her cosy cabin on 'C' deck, or in secluded corners of the otherwise deserted open decks, where a star-studded sky and balmy breezes added to the romantic atmosphere.

This gentleman had taken the trouble to engage both Priestleys in conversation from the outset, to strike up a friendship and to woo Edith with wit and a certain gruff charm. He had helped create their expanding circle of friends as the voyage progressed and persuaded

Edith to emerge from her 'maiden aunt' shell.

Edith had known about Jennifer's party-going and, in turn, Jennifer had known about Edith's budding romance. She was enjoying herself, keeping out of her aunt's way, and drawing attention away from her, all at the same time.

I have, of course, changed the ladies' names to protect their reputations, and would not presume to identify the gentleman involved.

All I will say is that, a few months after that trip, 'Puffer' Bradshaw bought a house near Shepton Mallet and pretty much gave up travelling entirely. Apart, that is, from taking the occasional cruise with his new wife and her niece.

From the reports that reached me, they particularly enjoyed themselves in the evenings. All the more so after that niece became engaged to a rather dashing ship's doctor. But that, as they say, is quite another story...

'Sinkers'

Do you have a problem with bits of useless information that stick in your memory and simply won't go away? A long-dead comedian's catch phrase, the words of a song, an old advertising slogan or jingle: the brain gets cluttered up with all manner of inconsequential stuff which refuses to budge.

I wish I could forget the lyrics of the Club Song we sang when I was a kid at the cinema on long ago Saturday mornings – absorbing all those cartoons and Westerns, and then singing lustily, accompanied by the manager at the Wurlitzer organ with its flashing lights and thumping chords. I wish I didn't know all the Shipping Forecast areas, in order, from Viking to Southeast Iceland, let alone those of the Inshore Waters.

I wish I didn't know that, in the heyday of the colonial civil service, Hong Kong, Rangoon and Singapore were known as 'Honkers, Rankers and Sinkers'.

I can't for the life of me remember who told me that last one. It was probably dear old Kenneth Westcott Jones – something of a legend among the fraternity of Fleet Street travel hacks who carved out the post-war trail that so many others were to follow. There were several such legends, whose names ring no bells outside our ranks – and are increasingly being forgotten within those ranks as time takes its toll. But don't get me started down that road.

Let me, instead, tell you about my visits to Singapore, or 'Sinkers', over the years.

In the early days it was an easy-going, relatively chaotic and raffish sort of place, because the tight hand of authority in the shape of Lee Kuan Yew and his modernising colleagues had yet to get a grip and start demolishing and rebuilding and generally cleaning up its act. (Years ago, you used to find a strip of paper laid across the top of the lavatory in your American hotel room. 'Sanitized for your personal convenience', it read. That slogan summed up the intention of Singapore's government.) Go there nowadays and you can visit 'The Bugis Street Experience' – a Disneyfied version of the old reality. However, it is the reality I remember with great affection.

Bugis Street came into its own late at night, when you could buy very large bottles of Tiger Beer which you drank as you sat at pavement tables and – in the words of the great travel writing cliché – 'watched the world go by'.

What a world it was. Vendors worked the tables flogging drinks and snacks, battery operated toys and sex gadgets. Small boys challenged you to games of noughts and crosses. They never lost – because they knew how to make the game a draw if they saw you were likely to win. And as the evening wore on and the beers took their toll, they regularly won. For them, it was a matter of patience and persistence.

But it wasn't the vendors or the small boys winning coins, or the generally louche atmosphere that drew tourists to Bugis Street. It was the nightly parade of 'shims' – or she-hims, 'ladyboys', who would suddenly appear as if by magic. They were immaculately dressed, poised and undeniably statuesque. They walked among the tables and posed for photographs, for which one was expected to pay a modest fee.

Today we know a great deal more about those who are 'transgender', certainly enough to sympathise with their circumstances. Back then it was all very different, and all very strange. Try as one might, one could not work out why these men were driven to dress and act as women. Why, indeed, they chose to parade every evening in Bugis Street. Though we were on a filming trip, we decided not to film there. However, chaps with Polaroid cameras accompanied the 'girls', taking their pictures as they posed beside you, and selling the prints.

It was raucous and raunchy and certainly not a location to which you would take your maiden aunt. But late one evening – or rather, in the small hours of one morning – I came to realise it had its serious side.

Most of the tourists had departed, and the restaurants and bars were closing up. There were four of us at our table, one of whom was our production assistant, the only girl in our party. She had struck up a conversation with a couple who had come to sit at the next table – a couple of the 'girls'.

Within a few minutes we were all conversing, and discovering more about their world in the shadows. Learning that, for most of them, the nightly parade and show was a means of earning the money they needed for the final operation that would complete their transformation.

'Not here in Singapore,' explained one – a strikingly attractive brunette. 'There are specialists in Thailand, so most of us go to Bangkok.' And there were other places, too, he added.

Yes, 'he', for in spite of the dress, the long hair, the perfect make up and the obvious 'enhancements', I had to regard the person I was talking to as a man rather than the woman he so much longed to be. You see, he had mentioned in passing that only a few years previously he had been a flight sergeant in the New Zealand Air Force. For obvious reasons, he could never return to his home and family in a small community on the South Island. For him, 'the land of the long white cloud' was lost forever.

I'm truly sorry the real Bugis Street has gone, for it was an essential part of the real Singapore. As were the death houses in Sago Lane.

That particular street, and a few others around it, was the heart of Singapore's funeral industry. It was lined with workshops making coffins of all styles and sizes. Straightforward caskets, of course, but also coffins in the shape of cars or planes or whatever else a grieving family might desire.

Other shops produced the paper 'money' to be burnt, along with all manner of paper goods which would be needed in the afterlife. When we roamed along Sago Lane, filming as we did so, I couldn't help thinking of ancient Egypt, and how the Pharaohs were interred with similar representations of their worldly goods.

The most interesting aspect of Sago Lane, however, was the 'death houses' – apartments located on the upper floors for elderly tenants. I was told it was the custom, when old people were clearly approaching their demise, for their relatives to move them into a convenient apartment where they could watch the busy street and get used to the idea that it would soon be their turn to occupy one of those magnificent coffins.

Looking up at the gnarled, walnut faces at those windows, I saw nothing but happy smiles. Which was odd.

Raffles, the most famous hostelry in Singapore, in fact one of the most famous in the world, used to be known as the 'Queen of Hotels', though when one looked at some of the distinguished chaps who regularly stayed there, a reversal of that slogan would be equally applicable. It was our billet on that first visit, and a very comfortable one, too.

But it had eventually to be dragged out of the 19th century and was completely refurbished and modernised, and as a consequence is not the grand old place it used to be. Still, it now has air conditioning, which is progress, I suppose. And much like today's sanitized version of Bugis Street, nowadays people who cannot afford to stay in the hotel may invest in a guided tour called 'The Raffles Experience', so turning it into a tourist destination.

My most recent visit to Sinkers came at the end of a rail journey which began in Bangkok. Because we travelled on local trains, choosing to stop off every now and then to film, the journey took several days, so by the time we arrived in Singapore we were all in the mood to wind down and relax in well-earned comfort, which we did.

However, the director – the same chap who had instigated the white water rafting in Switzerland – had another of his bright ideas. As an angle to our Singapore segment, he said we should sample the services offered by one of its health food restaurants.

At the time, as I recall, there was a strong 'healthy eating' movement back at home, and his idea was to show how this was managed in Singapore. Unfortunately, the concept of health food there is nothing like the concept of health food in Britain. But we were not to know this, as we made our way to the recommended eatery.

As the reporter, I was to be the guinea pig for this culinary experiment. So I sat myself down at the table and waited as the lights and the camera were sorted out so our filming could begin.

The first thing that happened was the head waiter ushering a pleasantly smiling chap to the table and introducing him as the restaurant's resident doctor. His job was to look at my eyes and my tongue and take my pulse (at three pressure points, not just the one we use at home). He also asked a couple of personal questions which we need not dwell on; and as a result of all that, he could diagnose what was wrong with me and what food I would be prescribed.

He told me, correctly, that I had slightly low blood pressure, slightly high cholesterol, and a tendency towards stiffness of the joints that would, one day, become arthritis. (He was right about that, too.) He rattled out a string of orders to the head waiter, who passed them on to a couple of minions. Then they all rushed away – the doctor to attend to another table, and the minions to prepare the grub I was to eat.

They brought me, first, a portion of fish – tilapia, I think – accompanied by a small salad and a handful of pine nuts. The cameraman filmed me as I took a couple of mouthfuls. So far, so good.

Then they brought four small pieces of toast, each bearing a scorpion. A real scorpion; dead, of course; and deep fried, if you want the exact details.

'I'm expected to eat this?' I asked plaintively, pointing out that the scorpions' stings were curled upwards in a very menacing fashion.

'It will make a great sequence,' replied the director. Camera and Sound said nothing. I suspect they were having trouble suppressing their laughter.

Realising I was beaten, I shrugged my shoulders, waited for the director to call 'action', picked up a slice of toast, and took a bite of it and its cargo. Then I delivered a comment to the camera along the lines of having enjoyed a long and unforgettable journey – one that had a sting in its tail.

When I finished, the others burst into laughter. I couldn't see what was funny.

'We'll have to do that again,' the director said eventually. 'When you did that piece to camera, you had the tail end of a scorpion stuck up your right nostril.'

Morocco Bound

I travelled frequently to Morocco during my early years as a professional globetrotter, mainly because several holiday companies promoted it as an 'exotic' destination.

Between ourselves, it's about as exotic as my Auntie Edna's winceyette nightgown, but the brochure copywriters did their work well, scattering the pages with 'Come with me to the Casbah' prose, and photographs of camels and belly dancers and the shifting, whispering sands of the desert. If you added in two quick choruses of 'One Alone', the whole Sigmund Romberg/Rudolph Valentino fantasy was yours for the taking – after you'd shelled out the appropriate number of guineas, of course.

(Oh yes, in those delightful dear old days, the tour firms priced their offerings in guineas, believing it gave them a professional image among the general public – much like solicitors. In this they were sadly mistaken.)

On an early visit, having developed a taste for mint tea, I joined a tour group for an afternoon trot around Tangier, but was disappointed to be taken to an establishment which advertised – in English, of course – 'Tea as Mother makes (we heat the pot)'.

Posters all over town promoted another restaurant with the promise that customers would have an opportunity to meet the owners 'Leo and Tessie from Warwick'.

Back in the hotel I tackled the tour rep about this, expressing my opinion that Morocco clearly lacked any 'exotic' element. I knew the brochures always exaggerated, but felt that a *soupçon* of something different should be on the cards. She instantly invited me to join her group for that evening's excursion into town.

'This is our most successful trip,' she declared. 'And it's a success because of its very special and very unusual element. I guarantee you won't be disappointed again.'

I decided to give her one more chance to set my pulse racing with that exotic element of Morocco that had so far eluded me. But it was not a promising start.

I joined a coach load of Brits who were, in the main, of mature years – though I have to say that at that stage of my career and, indeed, my life, I considered forty to be extremely mature, if not on the verge of decrepitude. My opinion, as you would expect, has changed with the passage of time.

Anyway, the coach took us on a short trip around the by-now familiar sights of Tangier before depositing us on the edge of the Medina. Our local guide and the rep led us through dark and narrow streets to that evening's destination, where we were to drink and dine and be ethnically entertained.

The restaurant was pretty much what I had expected, with carpets on its floors and walls, along with masses of tiles, most of which were brightly and elaborately decorated. Cushions had been placed on low benches and chairs alongside equally low tables. The robed staff wafted through our ranks, offering a selection of hors d'oeuvres and glasses of rough red wine, while a group of similarly robed musicians sawed and blew their way through a selection of apparently identical tunes, though their abilities were little appreciated by the visitors.

As everyone settled down to eat, I noticed that most were declining the offer of a second glass of wine. I did not blame them. Morocco isn't exactly noted as a wine-producing country, and I assumed the glasses contained a cheap import, possibly from France. Whatever its origin, it was not to my taste, nor that of my companions.

The meal was served with great flourishes. Industrial sized tajines were placed before us, containing a sort of stew whose meat content was unidentifiable. Large platters of vegetables were brought to the tables. Everyone tucked in heartily as the evening progressed.

The musicians took a break, then returned to provide a new selection of livelier tunes which heralded the appearance of the belly-dancer. She was, like her audience, of mature years, but she definitely knew her stuff and was applauded vigorously.

She maintained her scantily-veiled dignity, even when having to do that bit where a volunteer from the audience is dragged up to join her. I suspect the local guide, tipped off by the rep, had told her to steer well clear of me and pick, instead, the fat chap from Liverpool who saw himself as the joker in our pack (there's always one).

His efforts were greeted with ecstatic applause, and I noticed that, as they heartily demolished their dinner, the group seemed to have shed most of their inhibitions – or their 'British reserve' as we tend to label it. Many took to the dance floor gyrating in belly-dancer fashion (not a pretty sight) or cavorting about haphazardly. Voices were louder, laughter and cheers more frequent. They gave all the appearances of being drunk, but I knew that could not be so, as hardly any wine had been consumed.

I watched, in astonishment, as they formed a Conga line and, led by the belly-dancer, wove their way around the tables. There was singing, too – though, as is always the way, nobody knew all the words. The Hokey Cokey was attempted, but ended with a lot of people falling over.

This air of general merriment and well-being continued as our guide led us back to the bus through those dark and narrow streets, and during the ride back to the hotel. Once there, many made for the bar, reluctant to end the party.

At breakfast, when most people were nursing what would in other circumstances be hangovers, I tackled the tour firm's rep.

How did she account for the fact that it had been such a successful evening, when we both knew that wine had played no part in it. Was it, perhaps, that 'exotic' element she had promised? And if so, what the hell was it?

Making sure she could not be overheard, she confessed that an exotic touch had, indeed, been added to the proceedings. As was common back then – and for all I know is still common – Moroccan chefs used a little 'hasheesh' as a herb to spice up their offerings. As they tucked into their dinner, that usually sedate group of British holidaymakers, and yours truly, had got mildly stoned. As similar groups did every evening.

'Do you ever tell them?' I asked.

'Good Lord, no,' she said. 'If they knew, some of them might feel obliged to complain. As it is, they all have a good time and are none the worse for it.'

Though it happened, as I said, many years ago, I often think of that evening in Tangier, especially when I read about the campaign by 'mature' people to legalise the use of marijuana to relieve the pain of arthritis.

Down the years I visited Tangier frequently, usually staying at the Rif hotel, whose manager was a splendid fellow named Aimé Serfati.

He was a tall and elegantly dressed individual with a touch of the Omar Sharif about him. As Omar Sharif was yet to appear on the screen, he had the field very much to himself, to the obvious delight of foreign ladies staying in the hotel – with or without their husbands, it seemed to make little difference. Aimé, however, was a model of professionalism, keeping his private life very much apart from his work, and behaving like the perfect gentleman he was, thus ensuring that his lady guests – and, more importantly, their husbands – would have no cause to reproach him.

On one occasion, when I was there with a group of fellow hacks, he mentioned that the Swiss owner of the hotel was about to arrive and had invited all of us to dine as his guests, in his favourite restaurant.

'Is it the best restaurant in Tangier?' one of my companions asked.

'The best restaurant in Tangier is in this hotel,' Aimé swiftly and smoothly replied. 'But the one we are going to this evening has an atmosphere that he likes. There is nowhere else like it, I can assure you.'

A convoy of limousines conveyed us to a nondescript back street – of which Tangier has plenty. We tumbled out to find ourselves in front of a large room, brightly lit and open directly on to the pavement, having no front wall – rather like a garage or 'lock up'. It was filled with long tables and equally long benches, rather tightly packed, and we were invited to take our places.

Wine appeared. Much better wine than had been offered during that evening in the Medina. We sat and sipped and took in our surroundings. The floor appeared to be of hard packed sand, with no carpets or other coverings whatsoever. The white tiled walls were decorated only by large and very faded photographs of Hollywood film stars: Bette Davies, Judy Garland, Betty Grable, Humphrey Bogart, Gary Cooper, John Wayne, and many others, not all of whom we were able to identify, but clearly, all taken at the beginning of their careers.

As I examined the photographs I noticed a few cockroaches scuttling over them. But as nobody else commented on that, I thought it best to say nothing. Clearly this was a place full of character. Well, it had to be to attract the likes of our host, didn't it?

The food appeared. We had no choice, save what was placed before us. It was magnificent. I presumed a cockroach-infested kitchen lay somewhere behind the room in which we sat, for the waiters appeared through a pair of swing doors in the rear wall – doors that looked for all the world as if they belonged on the front of a Western saloon.

We ate well and drank moderately and had a brilliant time. I asked for the name of the restaurant and was promised I should have it when I returned to the Rif. That promise went unfulfilled. Two days later I attempted to make my way back to the nondescript street, but was unable to find it, much less the restaurant.

Though I tried on subsequent visits, I was never able to locate it, and have come to believe it never really existed and that the unforgettable meal in such good company never happened either. Sometimes life is like that.

✈

I find Marrakesh an exciting place, if only for its magnificent main square, which comes to life each evening. The city has some very smart hotels, too, more now than when I first went there.

Back then the jewel was the Mamounia Hotel, at which everyone who was anyone had been a guest. At the drop of a hat the hotel would trot out those names, the implication being that, lacking their fame, you were jolly lucky to be allowed to occupy one of its rooms – albeit that your accommodation was a far cry from the magnificent suites they had been allocated.

Once, I stayed in the Mamounia with my wife – and with a bunch of fellow hacks and their respective wives, too. The occasion was an 'inaugural', which was a regular fixture in our travel schedules all those years ago.

British European Airways, as it was then, was in the habit of inviting us to join the first flight to a new destination, or if not exactly the first at least one of the earliest ones. They needed publicity for their new routes, and we were the most efficient way of providing it.

However, they played the game very brilliantly. At a certain point in the year the selected travel writer received a telephone call from the secretary to the airline's senior public relations officer, the purpose of which was to fix a date for 'a nice little lunch'. Came the day and Humphrey would be the perfect host. One talked of this and that, of here and there. One asked how the other was getting on, pontificated about the state of the airline industry, the travel trade and the world in general.

Then, just as the 'nice little lunch' was drawing to a close, Humphrey would produce a list of new destinations to which the airline would be flying during the coming twelve months. 'Just cast your eye over that and let me know which ones you and your wife would like to go to,' he would say, as he rose to leave. 'Take your pick.'

That evening Sheila and I would go through the list, choosing the three or four which caught our fancy. And during the next few days I would ring my opposite numbers on other papers – who were, along with their wives, old friends (most national newspaper travel editors were men; the exceptions were Adrienne Keith Cohen of *The Guardian* and Alice Hope of the *Telegraph*, both mature ladies and confirmed spinsters). 'Have you had your lunch with Humphrey?

Which destinations have you chosen? Oh, yes, so have we. No, we didn't fancy that one, either.' That, roughly, was the gist of our conversations.

And so it came to pass that 'the gang' would take those lovely trips, in company with Humphrey and his wife. There was no question of being asked to write anything, for Humphrey wouldn't be so crass as to bring up the subject. But one did write, of course.

Which brings me back to Marrakesh, where Humphrey and his good lady were occupying one of the suites and keeping open house. 'Don't forget, come to our place for drinks before dinner' was more of a command than an invitation.

Apart from myself, the travel editors of *The Daily Express*, *The Daily Mail*, *The Guardian* and *The Sun*, as well as a senior staff travel writer from *The Daily Telegraph*, were in the party – with their spouses, if they had them. (It was an unwritten rule that one never brought anyone other than one's spouse on Humphrey's 'little trips'.) It would take a miracle to get such a group together nowadays, but back then we were more of a pack, being genuine friends as well as keeping an eye out for each other.

The basis of our friendship, incidentally, was that, as journalists who spent a lot of time away from our offices, we were liable to be undermined during our absences by jealous colleagues or penny-pinching managers, and thus needed friends to watch our backs. This may appear paranoid, but Fleet Street was something of a jungle, and I was glad of those friends. That Fleet Street is long gone, which is just as well – it was getting so competitive that people were stabbing each other in the chest.

On this occasion at the Mamounia in Marrakesh, we occupied a room underlooking the garden – yes, 'underlooking', for we were just below ground level in a room with a wall that sloped outwards and up to a reinforced glass ceiling. It was, notwithstanding, a very nice base for our sojourn, and we proceeded to make the most of it, and the superb facilities offered by the hotel.

What makes this trip memorable was the coincidental presence in the hotel of a lady named Barbara Hutton, and her extensive entourage. Invariably described in the gossip columns as 'the tragic Woolworth heiress', this immensely rich and immensely sad lady, then in her mid-fifties, was constantly pursued by packs of photographers who, although not yet known by the term paparazzi, along with unscrupulous reporters were eager to dish the latest dirt. Despite her wealth she had endured a ghastly childhood and her adult life had been marked by a series of disastrous marriages. The only husband who really loved her for herself and not her money was the film star Cary Grant, but even that marriage didn't last.

As soon as her 'people' knew of our presence, they went into a bit of a spin, fearing the worse. However, the urbane Humphrey made contact, assuring them that we were a merry band of travel hacks, interested only in the hotel and the city, and had no desire whatsoever to intrude on Miss Hutton, much less write anything about her.

It must have been difficult for them to accept this, but they did, though continuing to regard us with perhaps understandable suspicion.

Around mid-morning, having presumably breakfasted in their suites, Miss Hutton and her entourage would assemble beside the swimming pool. An advance party arranged chairs and loungers, occupying the outer ring and allowing later (and presumably more important) arrivals to occupy seats nearer the centre. Sometimes Miss Hutton – clearly in a fragile state of health – would be carefully and closely escorted to the heart of the group and settled gently on to a sunbed. There, her face hidden behind very large sunglasses, she would sit motionless.

So our two groups co-existed, exchanging polite nods of greeting across the swimming pool each morning. After a couple of days, and at the instigation of our wives, we engaged in some cautious fraternising with junior members of the entourage.

It was from one of them that I got a story which, of course, I never wrote.

I said that Miss Hutton was a sad figure, and this is no more than the literal truth. I saw no reason to add my twopennyworth of gossip about her, which is why I never published what would have been something of a scoop back then. But the sad lady has long departed this world, as, I suspect, have most of her Mamounia entourage. So, decades late, here is my 'scoop' – for what it's worth.

Barbara Hutton had a serious drug problem – a very serious drug problem. A string of specialists had tried a variety of treatments to rid her of the habit, but all failed because of the difficulty she, like all addicts, had in going 'cold turkey'. I have, thankfully, never taken any drugs (apart from that evening in Tangier!) but I am told that the withdrawal symptoms are horrendous.

However, among Miss Hutton's entourage was a French doctor who had come up with a cunning plan to overcome this. It was, briefly, to turn her from a drug addict into an alcoholic, so drink would alleviate the pain of coming off the drugs. Once she was drug-free, the doctor reasoned, it would be an easier task to wean her off alcohol. At the time of her encounter she was in the middle of this 'treatment'.

The way in which I was given this information – indeed, the way in which I have just written it down – makes Miss Hutton out to be something of a 'lab rat', a creature being used for an experiment. Her fragile personality and her dignity were disregarded in the pursuit of a 'cure'; which, as far as I am concerned, merely added to the sadness of her situation.

They were all still lounging around the swimming pool when we left for London. I was not particularly interested in gossip columns or the people who are featured in them, so I have no idea if her quality of life was at all improved by the machinations of the French doctor. But it seems perhaps not, as it has been said that in later life, her daily diet comprised twenty bottles of Coca-Cola with spirits, usually vodka, along with 'intravenous megavitamin shots mixed with amphetamines, a soybean compound, cigarettes, and a cocktail of drugs, including codeine, Valium, and morphine' (*The Daily Mail*).

People frequently say: 'I bet you've met some famous people during your travels.' I have, and sometimes I have encountered people who are famous for all the wrong reasons – and remember them vividly, even though we exchanged neither word nor glance.

✈

King Hassan II of Morocco was not a nice man. This is not my opinion, but that of many close observers of the monarch and his kingdom. They are the sort of worthy folk who study in detail the history and habits, the culture and the customs of various countries. They know things we travel writers do not, for we are 'here today, gone tomorrow' visitors, anxious only to bring away snapshot impressions for our readers – or listeners or viewers – who are, as holidaymakers, similarly interested in little beyond the quality of the food and wine and the standard of service in the hotels, the restaurants and the beach bars.

According to those experts, Morocco was not a happy place when Hassan II occupied its throne. But none of that concerned me when, sometime in the very early 1960s, I travelled there as a member of a small press group. The trip had been organised by a London-based public relations company who were being paid to promote an aspect of Morocco which now completely escapes me.

What I do know is that when we set off from Heathrow, the PR firm was represented by a young lady who turned out to know nothing of relevance about Morocco and was only on the trip in order to spend time with her boyfriend, who had been introduced to us as a freelance writer, but who was patently nothing of the sort.

Being with him meant she neglected her duties towards us, but this became irrelevant on the morning of the third day when news reached us that the pair of them, having commandeered one of the hire cars for an evening away from our prying eyes, had crashed on their way back to the hotel and were now in hospital.

Our Moroccan hosts were very concerned, but we assured them that, as long as the couple were receiving treatment for their injuries – fortunately, not serious – we were quite capable of continuing our tour without them. Arthur Eperon went so far as to suggest we would actually be better off without them, which I felt was a little callous. It was true, but nevertheless, perhaps it was an opinion best kept to oneself.

So we continued the tour – we being Arthur, Alice Hope of *The Daily Telegraph*, a freelance writing for one of the travel trade magazines, a young photographer named Charles, and me. An old Etonian, Charles, in his early twenties, was not long down from Oxford and working for a travel magazine – whether as a staffer or a freelance, I did not know. It was he, inadvertently, who brought about what we later referred to as 'the little contretemps'.

King Hassan – you'd almost forgotten him, hadn't you? – had been on the throne for about a year, possibly less. At the time the only thing I knew about him was that he had a couple of wives whom he had married in 1961, the year of his accession.

When we pitched up in Rabat, Morocco's capital was in the middle of some sort of royal celebration. Whether the shindig was for the king himself, or some other member of the royal family, I do not recall, but there was definitely a lot of partying going on and, as it was royal partying, dear Alice thought we should be included in it.

The readers of *The Daily Telegraph* would be short-changed if their representative in Rabat was not invited to the festivities, she argued. Which meant, of course, that the rest of us would have to go with her.

Arthur and I, along with the freelance writer, were not keen. Charles thought it might be rather fun, and provide an opportunity for some interesting photographs.

Alice railroaded us into agreeing, so we duly trotted along to the palace and were admitted. The place was crowded with high-ranking Moroccans, most of the diplomatic corps and assorted other VIPs. They seemed to be having a good time, so we mingled as best we could, making our individual progress from room to room.

After about a quarter of an hour, I sensed that something was not right. Lots of palace minions were hurrying about, most of them looking like they'd swallowed a wasp. There was a small amount of tumult, then the order came that all the journalists should leave. Immediately.

It wasn't just our little group, of course. Lots of proper journalists were in attendance, having been invited because they were far more likely than we to provide favourable propaganda for the Moroccan royals. But something had happened to make all of us personae non grata, and out we had to go. And the chaps who did the ejecting weren't subtle. A girl from *Paris Match* was pitched down a flight of steps and a lot of blows landed on local reporters and photographers.

Back in the hotel we wondered, as you would, about what had happened. But we did not wonder for long, because one of our local hosts appeared, anxiety writ large upon his features. And in a state of panic, too.

The press had been ejected, he explained, because someone had taken a photograph – an unauthorised and unacceptable photograph – of the king's mistress. A French lady, she was classified as a State Secret, as the populace at large would be most upset to discover their monarch was cheating on both his wives with a foreigner.

'Oh, crumbs,' said Charles. 'I think that might have been me.'

He explained how, proceeding through the various palace rooms, he had noticed a group of ladies sitting together in an ante chamber. They were most attractive ladies, so Charles had seized the moment, wielding the Hasselblad to good effect, and snatching a picture. He had no idea who they were, or that the lady in the centre of the group was a very special friend of the king.

'Where's the photograph?' demanded Arthur.

'Still on the roll of film in the camera,' replied Charles.

'In your bedroom?'

'Yes.'

'Right,' said Arthur decisively. 'Let's go.'

We all scampered up to Charles' room and within a few minutes the roll of film had been removed from the camera, replaced with a new one and Charles instructed to take a few photographs so the replacement roll would be as much used as the original. The removed film was carefully put into a canister which Arthur pocketed. Then we all hurried back down to the hotel lounge.

We were sitting around, trying to look nonchalant, when the security chaps turned up. They browbeat our Moroccan minders before turning their attention to us. As Arthur had anticipated, they demanded Charles's camera, and all his exposed films.

They got their wish, with Charles protesting just enough to convince them he was most annoyed, but not so much as to get a clip round the ear or a night in the cells. Then followed a few days of sheer enjoyment on our part, and massive frustration on the part of the fuzz.

Having processed the film in the camera, and all the others Charles had handed over, they realised the undeveloped film they were after was still in our possession.

They returned to the hotel, but we changed tactics and refused to be browbeaten, insisting that we had handed over all the exposed films, and pointing out that we had the wherewithal to splash their bullying ways all over the British press, to expose their harassment of innocent hacks who had, let it be noted, been invited to their country for the sole purpose of encouraging others to visit and bring much-needed foreign exchange. Alice did her dowager duchess act to great effect, so the heavies retreated to consider their next move.

Their next move was predictable: to search our rooms when we were absent. They didn't make too much of a mess, presumably being ordered not to give us further cause for grievance. But their searches were fruitless, for the canister of film remained with us at all times. They followed us, of course, but as they seemed incapable of removing their sunglasses, they were easy to spot. In any case, the canister was handed from one member of the group to another at frequent intervals.

It was, as I recall, snugly concealed about Alice's person when we finally boarded the plane for London along with the PR girl and her boyfriend, who had re-joined us, still heavily bandaged from their midnight encounter with a traffic light.

A couple of weeks later I saw Charles at a travel trade function and asked him if he had managed to sell the photograph to one of the London tabloids. After all the trouble we had gone to, I figured he owed us a pint or two from whatever fee he had obtained.

'I'm afraid it didn't come out,' he said. 'The light wasn't terribly good, but I took a chance. Got the exposure all wrong, though.'

I had never met Charles before that trip to Morocco, and after the last encounter, I never saw him again. However, he had a distinctive surname, which I have just used in my laptop's search engine. I now know that he went on to achieve considerable success and no little distinction. In the highly unlikely event that he reads this, I want him to know how much I enjoyed the pleasure of his company when our paths fleetingly crossed, and that for more than half a century, I have relished the memory of this story.

The Big Apple Corpse – and other Manhattan Memories

New York is a city about which its visitors have strong feelings. Love it or loathe it (and I have done both), it will make an impact. It is impossible to be indifferent to the Big Apple.

I write elsewhere about my very first visit to the USA, and how, in New York, I was press-ganged into becoming a tour guide. The fact that I managed to carry it off was due, in great part, to the confidence instilled into me by the driver of my allotted tour bus – a New Yorker from the soles of his glistening black shoes to the glowing tip of his cigar.

'Stick to the script, Johnny,' he advised me over our first breakfast together. 'Stick to the script and if they ask you something you don't know then, hell, just make it up. They'll never know the difference, and by the time they find out you weren't exactly on the level, you'll be long gone.'

Until I met Marvin, I had assumed Damon Runyon was exaggerating about the Guys and Dolls who inhabit his wonderful stories. But 'Big Marv' could have stepped straight from his pages. New York is lucky to have had such a chronicler. And Runyon was lucky to have had such a cast of real life characters to draw upon. I think today's vibrant London needs a modern-day Runyon to chronicle the words and deeds of its international cast of characters.

That first visit to the USA gave me hardly any time at all in New York. But I have plenty of stories from subsequent visits. About the

Pearly Kings and Queens who inspired the Macy's Morris Dance caper – which, alas, came to nothing. About the man who grazed his two shire horses in Battery Park. About the time we ended up singing opera in an Italian restaurant. I'll begin with the incident that gives this essay its title: the tale of the Big Apple Corpse.

It was a working trip, so I arrived in New York with a BBC film crew, all of whom save one were familiar travelling companions. The exception was the electrician, a somewhat taciturn fellow who had made it clear when we met at Heathrow that he didn't like America. He didn't like anywhere abroad, he added. And, therefore, he would not enjoy this trip.

So we knew where we stood with him, and made a mental note not to invite him to join us in any bar or restaurant, where the possibility of enjoyment might lurk. In fact, though, such a course of action would be impossible, for socialising together as well as working together is the only way to make filming trips successful.

This was some time in the mid 1970s, and it so happened that the BBC was going through one of its penny-pinching phases. As a consequence we were booked into a cheap hotel in an uptown location that was on the fringe of being dangerous. That we had no difficulty obtaining seven rooms in a busy tourist season should have sounded warning bells. However, according to the girl who made the bookings, it was a Holiday Inn, which was something – but not much – in its favour.

She must have been working from an out-of-date hotel directory, because the place was no Holiday Inn. It struck me instantly as being the sort of hotel which rents rooms by the hour rather than the day, and I suggested we might consider not checking in, but going somewhere else instead.

The director – a keen young man – dismissed my fears with a confident wave of his hand. He said something about not judging a book by its cover, so we trooped into the foyer, presented our group booking form and received our room keys from the bored blonde behind the reception desk. We unloaded our personal cases and equipment boxes from the minibus, then milled around for a while – reluctant to go much further into the fleapit.

Not so our electrician. He dived into the elevator, carrying his suitcase but leaving his equipment boxes in the foyer. The deal with 'gear' was that, if possible, it would be put into a secure store room so as to avoid cluttering up the bedrooms. That was usually arranged by the cameraman's assistant, and our electrician had decided to leave him to it.

We were still in the foyer, negotiating a rate for the use of the storeroom, when less than five minutes later the lift returned with the electrician in it – carrying his suitcase.

He dropped his room key on the desk in front of the bored blonde.

'There's somebody in my room,' he said.

'Can't be,' she drawled. 'According to the book, the guy in 426 checked out.'

'Oh, he's checked out, all right,' replied the electrician. 'He's dead.'

For the first time since our arrival, emotion registered on the blonde lady's face.

'Oh my gawd!' she exclaimed. 'D'ya think he's been murdered?' (She pronounced it 'moidud'.)

'I couldn't see any blood, he's lying in bed and there's a Do Not Disturb sign on the door,' said the electrician. 'I think it's probably natural causes.'

'Thank gawd,' said the blonde lady. 'A murder ['moidur'] would be real bad for our reputation.'

Within half an hour we had moved many blocks downtown into a better neighbourhood and a far better hotel. The electrician's opinion about 'abroad' being a terrible place had clearly been reinforced, but we made him join us for after-work drinks and meals, and I think he managed to enjoy himself a little. We took care not to mention the corpse.

✈

On subsequent trips, though I usually flew into New York, I arrived by sea using Cunard's *QE2* (*Queen Elizabeth 2*) on three occasions. One of those – sometime in the mid 1980s – saw me acting as chaperone and host to a group of ladies who were readers of one of the magazines for which I wrote travel articles.

We had put together a special offer – the trans-Atlantic crossing, followed by a week-long tour of the eastern USA and a flight home – and it was taken up eagerly by our readers, the overwhelming majority of whom brought along their husbands. However, a few ladies were travelling solo or in pairs, so I thought it best to keep more of an eye on them, leaving the husbands and wives to sort things out for themselves.

Coincidentally, an acquaintance (one of Fleet Street's most powerful travel editors) was also on the *QE2*, and it came about that he and I fell into the company of two of 'my' ladies. Both were divorced, one of them comparatively recently.

This latter lady swiftly formed a 'very close personal relationship' with my chum, which made life a tiny bit complicated, but they were both consenting adults, so I thought my best course of action was to let them get on with whatever it was they were getting on with. It meant I had to spend a lot of time with the other lady, but she proved to be a tolerant soul.

All went without major hitches until we reached New York, where the pilot managed to run us aground at the mouth of the Hudson. This caused a lot of consternation among passengers who were travelling on by train or plane and would certainly miss their connections. It caused particular consternation to my chum, whose wife had flown from Heathrow to meet her beloved at the quayside and whisk him away to the shops and the sights – but mainly the shops.

Unfortunately, he had omitted to mention his marital state to the lady on the *QE2*, which caused her to become exceedingly angry and exceedingly tearful in quick and repeating succession.

However, once we had managed to get ashore, I arranged to meet the ladies in our hotel bar, from where – much fortified by a strong concoction called Rusty Nail – we took a cab to one of my favourite restaurants – Asti's.

Asti's is, alas, no more, having closed its doors in early 2000. But it was a tremendous establishment, and exactly the place one should take a lady who has been wronged by a cad and in need of cheer. And, of course, the friend of the lady who has been wronged etc.

Located on East 12th street in Greenwich Village, Asti's was an Italian restaurant like no other. For one thing, most of its red-jacketed waiters were – or had been – professional opera singers. And opera was on the menu, along with every pasta dish known to man, an assortment of meat and fish dishes, salads as large as herbaceous borders, and an extensive wine list.

In the middle of serving you, the waiter was quite likely to down plates and join his fellows on a tiny stage for a rousing chorus or two, before resuming his waiting work. A handful of soloists belted out arias and duets, covering just about every operatic melody you have ever heard. And I do mean 'belted out', for Asti's entertainment was much like Asti's food and drink – full bodied and full blown with little room for subtlety. The singing was powerful and fun but not, to be blunt, of the highest quality.

Nevertheless, my ladies adored it. The wronged maiden came to her senses and, thanks to the healing power of much full-bodied Italian red wine, saw the funny side of her situation. She was not, after all, some lovesick young maiden with no experience of man's wicked ways. And she had to admit she had thoroughly enjoyed the high seas part of the adventure. At one point in the evening she threatened to provide graphic details of this, but we managed to persuade her that discretion was paramount in such matters. And poured out more wine.

So she did not object when a waiter took her from the table, dressed her in a voluminous cloak and stood her with other selected female diners who had to provide a background of humming while a couple of soloists knocked out yet another aria we all recognised. In my turn, I was clad in a monk's habit, given an electric 'candle' and joined fellow diners in yet another wild performance. I have absolutely no idea which opera has a chorus of candle-bearing monks (if any) but if there is one, that's the one we performed.

By the time I had escorted the ladies back to our hotel, some semblance of emotional order had been restored, and I felt sure they would enjoy the rest of their holiday.

I can't leave the subject of Asti's without mentioning an earlier visit. I had been told about the singing waiters, and the fact that sometimes the customers would include members of the chorus of the New York Metropolitan Opera, who would regularly pop into Asti's for a (discounted) meal and the chance to exercise their vocal cords.

On this occasion, I spotted a familiar face. Dining alone, at a table against the wall – which was, naturally, covered with scores of photographs of opera stars – was Peter Glossop, a well-known English baritone who was in New York for a series of performances at the Met. Peter was a Sheffield lad – born and educated in the city, who started his career with the Sheffield Operatic Society. Coincidentally, I had worked on the *Sheffield Telegraph*, its morning newspaper, and interviewed him a few times, latterly in London.

Figuring he would want to be left alone to enjoy his meal, I turned my attention back to the friends with whom I was dining. But a few moments later he was standing at our table, asking what the *Sheffield Telegraph* was doing in New York. I explained my new status as a travel writer, introduced him to my friends and asked after his wife, the mezzo-soprano Joyce Blackham (they divorced in 1977).

'Are you going to sing tonight?' I asked.

'Hadn't planned to,' he said. 'But I might.'

And he did. It was marvellous. Actually, it was a hell of a lot better than marvellous, and quite unforgettable.

Like Asti's, the Manhattan Brewing Company is no more, but it was an equally memorable location which we filmed on one BBC trip.

It was located in a disused electricity sub-station in Thompson Street, right at the bottom of Manhattan Island. Our cameraman described it as a dodgy neighbourhood, but the brewery was far from dodgy. Opened in 1984, it claimed to be the first new brewery east of the Mississippi since Prohibition, and was, unquestionably, the real deal.

Its cavernous interior housed half a dozen great copper vats which produced a pair of beers called Manhattan Amber (a bitter) and Manhattan Gold (a lager). I seem to recall there was also a very dark brew, a stout.

It served all of these beverages on draught in the bar, whose floor was covered in sawdust ('That was the furniture before last night's brawl,' somebody wisecracked).

There were dartboards and the kind of basic pub grub – meat pies and sausage rolls – that you would have found all over the UK in those long-ago days before the advent of 'gastro-pubs', and when America was a wasteland as far as decent beer was concerned. For those who took their ale seriously, the huge and dominant American brands were little more than fortified lemonade, and local micro-breweries were decades away. So this was a place of wonder.

Unfortunately, most of its young and trendy customers were unused to the strength of these brews. 'We have a few regular customers,' a bartender told me, 'but most people can't remember how to get back here after a session.'

Nevertheless the brewery was doing a roaring trade, and the owners – eager for more – were quite happy to have us film there in order to encourage visiting Brits to head for Thompson Street.

By chance, one of my daughters was in New York, with a girl friend, and the pair of them joined us that evening after we had finished filming. I watched with some amusement how they dealt with good-humoured attempts to chat them up. Then my daughter called me across to join them.

'I've heard some really original lines before now,' she said, 'but his takes some beating.' She indicated a young chap sitting with them.

He gave a shrug. 'It isn't a chat-up line,' he protested. 'All I asked was would you like to see my shire horses?'

'I suppose it makes a change from would you like to see my etchings?' I said. 'But if you do have shire horses, I'd certainly like to see them.'

So the young fellow – whose name, I think, was Mark – led us through the bar and the kitchens at the back, across a narrow alleyway and into a dark stable building.

There in the gloom was a pair of massive Clydesdale dray horses – the last thing you expect to encounter in New York.

He explained that the brewery had contracts with many bars in central Manhattan, and part of the deal was that beer would be delivered in the old-fashioned way, in oak barrels (imported from the Bass brewery in the UK) carried on a dray drawn by two horses (imported from Whitbread, also in the UK). What had started as a publicity gimmick had quickly become a much-admired part of the New York scene.

Though I am unsure about the young man's name, I do remember that the horses were Prince and Duke. And that they grazed every day in Battery Park.

✈

Another time, my wife and I found ourselves in New York over Thanksgiving weekend. This happened from time to time because my wife's birthday was 26th November, and we had got into the habit of celebrating it in the USA. Our usual plan was to spend a few days there shopping and sightseeing (but mostly shopping) before heading down to Orlando, where we had a house, for a change of scenery – and, more important, a change of weather.

So I have been in New York when the famous Macy's Thanksgiving Day Parade takes place. This is something many people know about from the heart-warming and jolly film *Miracle on 34th Street* – either the 1947 version starring Edmund Gwenn, or the 1994 remake, with Richard Attenborough in the role of Kris Kringle. However, in reality the parade is of great commercial significance, because the arrival of Father Christmas at Macy's store is the signal for the start of a sales campaign throughout the USA. From Thanksgiving Weekend until Christmas, the bells you hear jingling are those of the cash registers.

It is no surprise that Macy's takes massive care to organise a spectacle, with marching bands, an assortment of floats, all manner of entertainers built into the parade and great helium-filled balloons shaped as cartoon characters floating high above the marchers.

Because the weather is usually very cold, one sees strange sights that day. I recall the occasion when a huge posse of kilted bagpipers (possibly from the New York Police or Fire Department) swung past, and we spotted that every man was wearing a pair of flesh-coloured tights as well as the more familiar long socks.

But what is most important to this story is the fact that we also saw a group of twenty or thirty Pearly Kings and Queens marching past. Well, when I say marching past I should explain that, for reasons unknown to me, Macy's parade progresses in fits and starts, and the Pearlies were actually held up for a few moments right where we were standing.

We gave them a friendly greeting and a couple of Kings wandered over. One of them greeted me like an old mate, having seen me on television (which always helps break the ice). He explained they were from the outskirts of London and had been given permission to join the parade so as to provide an international flavour to the proceedings.

I couldn't get more information because, at that moment, the parade – and the Pearlies – moved on. But it planted a seed.

I was then – and still am – involved with a charity called The Family Holiday Association. Its aim is to provide modest holidays for people who desperately need a break but whose situation, as a result of illness, death, divorce, unemployment or other setbacks, means they cannot afford what most of us take for granted. The charity receives massive support from the much-maligned travel industry, all of which is given without publicity fanfares, staff going about their fund-raising tasks with equal modesty.

Anyway, having given the matter much thought, it struck me that if I could get Macy's to agree, we could introduce some Morris dancers into the parade, each of whom could be sponsored (just as you sponsor people in a 'fun run') in order to raise funds for the FHA.

I set to work to make it happen and, after a lot of time and effort, got to the situation where British Airways and Virgin Atlantic agreed to provide free or very cheap trans-Atlantic flights, and the English Folk Dance and Song Society promised to recruit around 100 Morris dancers (preferably husbands and wives, so as to minimise the cost of hotel rooms). The FHA would help them get sponsors. Morris dances are static displays, but I was assured that a moving Morris dance could be arranged so the stop-start parade would not be unduly delayed.

In case you think my plan was a foolish one, you might like to know that the English Folk Dance and Song Society sent a demonstration team to the USA in 1929, and that Morris dancing is popular from coast to coast. The city of New York has at least five 'rings': the Bouwerie Boys in Brooklyn Heights, the Greenwich Morris Men, the Half Moon Sword, the New World Sword and the Ring O'Bells (a predominantly female group and I have a feeling it used to be called the Ring O'Belles – but I may have got that wrong).

The stage was set. All that was needed was agreement from Macy's – specifically from the lady who then organised the parade. I began a correspondence with her. I sent her video tapes of Morris dancers. Then I went to New York and met her in her office at the world-famous store.

The meeting was a great success. She and her staff were charming and full of enthusiasm. Having discovered that Morris dancing was not an all-male pursuit – for that would have been a problem at a time when sex-equality was fresh on the social agenda – Macy's had warmed to my plan. I returned to London with very high hopes.

To this day I do not know what happened to make them change their minds. But change their minds they did, and New York was denied the spectacle of massed Morris dancers marching and prancing and generally cavorting merrily in the Thanksgiving Day Parade. Their letter was as courteous as they had been in person, but firm in its rejection.

Perhaps it is just as well, given how cold New York can be at that time of the year. Though warming tights – if worn at all – would have been concealed by white trousers, there is the possibility that the little bells strapped around those trousers might have become frozen and soundless.

And a Morris Dancer with silent bells is not to be tolerated.

The Odd Couple
a 'faction'

As I said before, I've a soft spot for an ancient vessel called *Ocean Majesty*, though I believe she no longer exists. I lectured on her for many years, enjoying the company of crew and passengers alike. And I well understand the attraction she had for those passengers. She wasn't the smartest of ships – 'It's only the rust that holds her together,' one cruise director observed. However, the atmosphere on board was excellent.

Character, they call it. Some ships have it, some never will. Though she was very small by today's standards, the dear old *Maj* had it in spades, and that comfortable and familiar ambiance kicked in as soon as she sailed from Tilbury. Most of her passengers were regulars, and I had the impression that those sampling her for the first time would be likely to return.

Not Ted Burgess, however. I don't think Ted liked cruising, but he had taken this trip at the behest of his wife, Pamela, who fancied it like crazy. She fancied the posh frocks and the formal receptions and the opportunity they gave her to flash the bling. For Pamela Burgess – far younger than the portly, fifty-something Ted – was what I believe is known as a 'trophy wife'. Having made big bucks, Ted was able to discard his first wife, marry again, and keep 'young Pammy', as he called her, in the style to which she aspired.

I didn't like Pamela Burgess. I didn't like Ted, either. They were not a likeable couple.

From the outset she made it her business to outshine every female passenger. Her dresses had to be newer and smarter than theirs. Her hair and make-up had to outclass their efforts (or, as far as the hair was concerned, the professional efforts of the girls in the salon on C deck).

As for the jewellery, well – young Pammy must have spent an awful lot of Ted's ill-gotten gains on assembling a mighty collection of rings and bangles, necklaces and brooches. She sparkled like a Christmas tree on every possible occasion.

Now I put 'ill-gotten gains' in that last paragraph, but don't want you to think I wrote those words just to be unpleasant. It quickly became pretty clear to me, and to a lot of other folk on the ship, that Ted had assembled his pile with scant regard for the finer points of the law and complete disregard for the unwritten rules of business, and of life, that we call 'fair play'.

The Burgesses came from Devon, some place west of Exeter whose name I forget. I do recall being told that they lived in a very large house in a very exclusive development which Ted's firm had constructed.

Oh, I forgot to mention that he was a builder. Or, rather, he was the owner of a very successful building company, having done his time as a bricklayer and plasterer and roofer and goodness knows what else. Having started from the bottom, Ted Burgess had made his way swiftly to the top using a combination of inborn cunning, sharp dealing and outright deceit.

You don't have to take my word for it. Every evening, jacket cast aside and tie and tongue equally loosened, he would hold forth in the midships bar about his many successes. To hear the way he told it, there were no failures in Ted's life. Other people suffered the failures.

It so happens that my son has had a successful career in the construction industry. Over the years I have learned from him the ways in which unscrupulous individuals can fudge the paperwork, cut corners and massage profits, as Ted Burgess clearly had.

During that cruise, some passengers would, for the sake of a few free drinks, listen to his bragging tales. Their presence encouraged him to spill a lot of beans that would have remained unspilled had he remained sober. Because I was in the habit of taking a nightcap with the cruise director in the same bar, I overheard several of Ted's tales.

He was, first off, a master at dealing with local council officials, who could be persuaded – in exchange for what he called 'a discreet little bung' – to turn a blind eye to his corner-cutting ways. He confessed to the habit of dispensing 'sweeteners' to local councillors in order to influence their decisions with regard to planning applications, and railed furiously against the regulations they were unable to ignore, no matter how much he pushed them. Such regulations were, as far as he was concerned, designed to do nothing else than make life hard for him and other enterprising local businessmen.

Ted truly believed that the rules the rest of us have to live by should not apply to him. He complained about the fees he had to pay his accountant in order to 'get the books looking good' for the benefit of anyone with a legitimate interest in examining them. Such people, in his words, were 'interfering busybodies' whose aim in life was to stifle enterprise. Enterprise was a word he used a lot.

His capacity for self-delusion was quite amazing. He would boast of his dodgy methods without turning a hair, for he simply could not acknowledge that he was doing anything wrong.

Added to all that was the presence of Pammy, who rattled on at every opportunity about her wonderful husband and all the gifts he had lavished upon her. She had a sharp tongue, too, and used it when speaking of his first wife – a woman she had never actually met.

Ted and Pammy were, someone remarked, absolutely made for each other.

So, as often happens, Ted and Pamela Burgess quickly became the passengers to avoid. People tried to sit as far as possible from them in the restaurant or on the excursion coaches. They scurried to a different corner of the bar when the Burgesses settled themselves down for an after-dinner session of booze and boastfulness. They gave them the cold shoulder. If you have ever been on a cruise – or, come to that, any kind of group holiday – you know this is nothing really out of the ordinary: the presence of people like the Burgess couple has that effect. It is worse if there are, say, just three dozen of you on a coach tour, infinitely less of a problem in a huge hotel or a vast super liner, where there is more opportunity to hide, more space to put between you and them. But *Ocean Majesty* was a small ship, so the couple were hard to ignore.

We were about three days out from Tilbury on the homeward run, when I noticed something rather odd. I spotted an elderly passenger named Parker talking to Mrs Burgess. They seemed to be having a very pleasant conversation, with Parker nodding and smiling and laughing gently at young Pammy's witticisms.

Edwin and Mabel Parker were a complete contrast to the Burgesses. I had fallen into conversation with them on the first evening of our voyage, and enjoyed their company on numerous subsequent occasions. They came to my lectures and were kind enough to say nice things about them – which made them extra-specially super people, as far as I was concerned, of course.

Edwin Parker was, I guess, in his mid-sixties. He had an air of quiet scholarship which made me think he might have been a schoolmaster, or even a university professor. When I enquired, however, he admitted to a   career in some unspecified government department – I got the impression it might have been the old Ministry of Agriculture. Whatever it was, he was obviously not keen to 'talk shop', and I decided this was probably because his career had not been the success he had hoped for.

Mabel had been a nurse in her youth, but had given up work when their children – two sons – had appeared on the scene. Once they were off her hands, she had worked as a librarian, but was now interested only in her grandchildren – and to her commitment to three days a week assisting in a charity shop.

That charity shop, it transpired, was in Budleigh Salterton, in Devon. So I assumed the fact that they lived in the same county was what had drawn Edwin into a conversation with Mrs Burgess.

That evening Ted Burgess and his glittering missus dined at the same table as Edwin and Mabel Parker. They had to suffer Ted's boastful accounts of his life and work, but I presumed they endured it through politeness and possibly because Ted had insisted on paying for the wine, although sensibly allowing Edwin the pleasure of choosing it.

For the last two days of the voyage Edwin Parker and Ted Burgess spent a lot of time in each other's company. Edwin seemed to be genuinely interested in what Ted had to tell him, though I couldn't for the life of me understand why. Was it, perhaps, because the old gent felt sorry for the unpopular pair? In any event, they made an extremely odd couple, if only because of their contrasting personalities.

Shortly after we had docked at Tilbury and were assembled in the main lounge to await disembarkation, I wandered among my fellow passengers, wishing them a safe journey home and expressing the hope that I might see them some time in the future.

Mrs Parker was there, but of Edwin there was no sign.

I sat beside her, intending nothing more than to exchange a few pleasantries before moving on. Edwin, she informed me, had gone in search of a cup of tea and, possibly, a biscuit. She smiled as she said it, obviously in a good mood.

So I took the plunge.

'I hope you don't mind me mentioning it, but I was a little surprised to see you in the company of Mr and Mrs Burgess,' I said.

'Oh, they are such ghastly people,' she replied. 'We avoided them for most of the cruise, but Edwin said he couldn't resist getting to know more about them. After all, the man is such an out-and-out swindler. Eating a couple of meals with them, and spending an hour or so in the bar afterwards was a small price to pay.'

I thought her last remark was an unusual way of putting it. 'A small price to pay for what?' I asked.

'Oh for all that information,' she said. 'And we exchanged addresses and telephone numbers, too.'

At that moment Edwin appeared, bearing a small tray with two cups of tea on it and smiling triumphantly.

'John was asking about our friendship with Mr and Mrs Burgess,' Mabel said, as he sat down in the seat I had vacated.

'Yes, I found him a most interesting fellow,' mused Edwin, as he sipped his tea. 'I'm really looking forward to our next meeting.'

'What on earth makes you say that?' I said in disbelief.

The gentle face looked up at me. The soft blue eyes twinkled. 'Did I not mention that I work for the Inland Revenue?' he said quietly. 'I'm what they call a compliance officer. I investigate people who don't pay their proper share of tax. Oh yes, I really am looking forward to my next meeting with Mr Burgess.'

Og the Wench

I've many fond memories of Iceland – and some of which I am not so fond – but, as it was the first destination I reported on for the BBC's *Holiday* programme, it occupies a special place in my thoughts.

At the start of that television series there were no location reporters. Tom Savage, the producer, travelled around with a film crew (it was film, way back then) and returned with pictures and some location sound. My job was to supply a commentary, relying on my own past experiences of the place – if it was somewhere I had visited under my own steam.

If, as happened more often than not, the locations weren't known to me, I had to work from notes brought back by Tom and his production assistant, and by cribbing stuff from relevant guidebooks. Talk about making bricks without straw!

My commentaries were handed over to Cliff Michelmore, whose voice would supply the essential element of BBC authority. Looking back at that first couple of years, I think we managed to pull it off, though at times it was touch and go.

When, in 1970, the idea was mooted of taking someone to report from the locations, I wasn't sure I'd be suitable. My background was purely as a print journalist, and I was still getting used to the hugely different discipline of writing for television. ('Writing to fit time rather than space', somebody once said, though there was a lot more to it than that.) Going to the destinations would certainly help with the writing, but I found the show business side of television more of an obstacle to journalism than anything else.

Well, cutting a long story relatively short, Tom said he would take me on a location, where I could see how the films were made and do one or two 'pieces to camera'. If everything worked out, I could then voice my own commentary. And if all went well I might graduate to being a reporter on location as well as a studio-based 'resident travel expert'.

The location he chose was, as you know, Iceland, and the subject of our film would be a 'safari' type of holiday into the spectacular heart of the island. The tours were organised by a chap named Ulfar Jacobsson, and were based on flights from New York on Loftleidair, an airline which, not being a member of the international cartel, undercut all the others.

So, basically, we were going to accompany a bunch of American cheapskates who thought that roughing it on a camping trip in Iceland was a really good way to spend their entire two-week holiday. Nonetheless, I had to agree it would make a stunning story, if only because of the landscapes through which we would be travelling. There was no way we could spare a whole two weeks, so once we had arrived in Reykjavik, we had to sort out the logistics.

It was quickly agreed we would travel with the group for the first four days, then leave them and fly back to Reykjavik in a specially chartered plane that would pick us up from an airstrip somewhere in the back of beyond.

We had to leave behind Prudence, our production assistant, and Ted the electrician, but they didn't mind when they saw the Americans – who were, to put it kindly, an eccentric-looking bunch – and the two vehicles in which we were to travel.

One, for the twenty or so clients, was a modified American school bus, painted a drab grey-green colour, but with bits of the original yellow showing through. I later confirmed that it had been acquired from the American Air Force base at Keflavík – I suspect with the connivance of a real-life Sergeant Bilko.

The other vehicle was a truck, about the same length as the bus, but modified to provide a large cabin for the driver and seven or eight passengers, while the canvas-covered rear was crammed with tents and trestle tables, folding chairs and all manner of food and drinks in boxes and bottles and cans.

The tour guide drove the bus. The truck was driven by a huge Icelandic bloke whose torso and arms bulged out of a check shirt and who smoked a pipe upside down. We thought it best not to comment on that.

There were two girls with him. One was, obviously, his girlfriend. The other, equally obviously, was not. This lass we christened Og the Wench.

She was a hefty girl, clad in a set of blue dungarees and with a check shirt similar to that worn by the driver. She had a round, expressionless face, which made it hard to estimate her age. I guess she would be in her late twenties – two or three years older than the driver's girlfriend. She was what my mother used to call 'homely'.

Now I know you shouldn't judge people by their appearance, but there was no getting away from the fact that nature hadn't been kind to Og. And no getting away from the fact that she was indifferent to the situation. She was certainly making no attempt to (in another of my mother's phrases) 'make the most of herself'.

Tom, Robin (sound), Roy (cameraman), Steve (assistant camera man) and I clambered into the cab and, fitting very snugly, we set off on the Icelandic Safari Adventure.

The peculiar thing about this girl – and the reason we nicknamed her 'Og' – was that she sat still and silent for most of the time, making no attempt to communicate either with us (which would have been understandable) or with her two colleagues (which was odd). In repose, her face had a grim, almost sullen, expression.

On the rare occasions when she felt it necessary to speak, she leaned towards either the driver or the other girl and mumbled slowly. We couldn't understand a word, of course, though I got the distinct impression that, had she been speaking English, we still would have been none the wiser.

The driver's girlfriend spoke a few words of English. He spoke only Icelandic. Og confined herself to her rare mumbles, though as the day and the journey wore on she occasionally responded with a squeal and a giggle to something the driver said to her. She didn't look at us, though I was sure that the driver's comments were about us, but I got the impression she would rather not have had our company.

Before I forget, I must tell you that 'Steve' is not the real name of our assistant cameraman. Apart from the fact that I have forgotten what it was – though I am absolutely certain it wasn't Steve – you will understand the reason for this as my tale unfolds.

From the outset the trip looked like living down to my expectations. We were hardly out of the Reykjavik metropolitan area before we left the proper road and began to bounce and shudder our way into the heart of the countryside. From the canvas-covered rear of our vehicle came a series of bangs and crashes as the rations and equipment settled into place. I dreaded to think how the Americans were managing.

After what seemed an eternity of jolting, with occasional stops to admire particularly fine views and for us to do some eager filming, we reached our first, isolated, destination. We all – including the Americans – pitched in to set up the tents, while the girls got to work cooking an evening meal, a very hearty stew. The BBC had been allocated two tents. Tom, Robin and I squeezed into one. Roy and Steve took the other, sharing it with our equipment.

Next morning we breakfasted in a howling gale. The wind was so strong it blew the Cornflakes out of the bowl unless you got the milk in quickly – allowing for the wind strength and direction as you poured.

Now this would have been a straightforward story of stoicism in the face of hardship, had it not been for Steve. But Steve fancied himself as a lady's man, and his problem was that the only available lady was Og.

He had checked out the Americans, quickly discovering they were overwhelmingly couples. The only single travellers were male, including two who wore fringed buckskin jackets and trousers, sported walrus moustaches, and were constantly talking about the West – the Wild West, of course – and the activities of such characters as Billy the Kid, Wild Bill Hickok and Buffalo Bill. (What was it with all these aggressive Willies?) Learning they both worked for New York City's Department of Sanitation was another object lesson in never judging by appearances.

Anyway, the point I wish to make is that, as far as Steve was concerned, Og was his only option. Under normal circumstances he would never have given her a second glance – probably not even a first glance – but circumstances were far from normal. He was fed up and far from home, and not one to back away from a challenge.

So he devoted most of the next day to wooing Og. It was a hard task, for she ignored him completely – to the extent of behaving as if he wasn't even there. But he persisted, turning on his South London charm at every opportunity.

As far as I could tell, it was doing him no good at all. As the day wore on, we stopped to allow the Americans to do their sightseeing and take photographs, while we filmed the scenery (and the Americans), and I made copious notes. Steve didn't shirk his duties, but seemed to have ample time to continue what was an exceedingly strange courtship. Quite apart from the language barrier, there was a wide gulf where any form of understanding might have occurred.

I did notice a flicker of acknowledgement when she accepted a cigarette, and also spotted that she was spending more time than usual in whispered conversations with the driver's girlfriend – and, occasionally, with the driver himself. On the second evening, as we gathered round the cooking pots for our meal, I noticed that Og was being particularly generous when she doled out Steve's mashed potatoes. I decided not to read anything of significance into this. But when she joined us, bearing her own well-stocked plate, and sat down beside Steve, we had to agree this was something of a breakthrough. We had absolutely no idea what it meant, but we decided Steve might be getting somewhere.

'I'd take care if I were you,' Tom said to Steve. 'We don't want to offend these people.'

Steve brushed aside his concern. As he saw it, Og was simply falling under the spell of his irresistible charm, and he, the great Lewisham Lothario, had everything under control.

In this he was wildly wrong, making the mistake of regarding Og in the same way as he regarded his many London girlfriends. She was not to be judged on that basis. She had her own rules.

During our final full day we worked hard to complete our filming, tracking the Americans as they waded through wide but shallow rivers and clambered over the rocky terrain to reach spectacular waterfalls and the like. This was my first experience of location filming and I learned that, though we sometimes needed to wait around until the light or the ambient sound were just right in order to get a particular shot, such times were rare and filming was done at a fairly rapid pace.

I also learned that the traditional task of the presenter (though I preferred the label of reporter) was to carry the camera tripod – or 'the legs'. It was a task I was to enjoy undertaking for the next thirty years, though I didn't know that at the time.

The story began to take shape in my mind. Until then I had fitted my commentaries to the edited films. Now I could note down ideas and phrases as I watched the film's sequences coming together. I could also share the satisfaction as, for example, Roy was able to capture the play of light and shade on landscape as clouds moved across the sky, or as Robin recorded the sound of swift water tumbling along a boulder-strewn river bed.

I was also able, at first with diffidence, to make suggestions about particular shots which I thought would help bolster the effect of my words – or, rather, the words that were beginning to gather in my thoughts.

There was no doubt this was going to be a pretty good story, so I began to feel a lot happier about my new role. However, beyond the confines of the work, there was little to be happy about.

At the end of that day, after the tents had been erected and the meal prepared, I noticed Og talking animatedly to the other girl, and gesturing towards Steve. They both looked very pleased with themselves.

'What was she saying to you?' I asked the driver's girlfriend after Og had left.

'Ah yes,' said the girl, with a very serious look on her face. 'She says she has make decision to sleep with him tonight. She is sad for him because he loves her much. She loves him not. But she wants to be kind.'

I took my bombshell to Tom, Robin and Roy. Together we broke the news to Steve.

'You've gone too far this time,' said Roy, who travelled a lot with Steve and knew how he behaved. 'There could be a lot of trouble over this.'

Steve brushed our fears aside. Grafted on to his character as a well-travelled 'man of the world', was all the arrogance of a twenty-something-year-old. He needed no guidance from us in the art of dealing with amorous females. As far as he was concerned Og's appeal lay in the challenge she had presented. He had no desire for conquest. Far from it.

After dinner, as on previous evenings, the whole party sat around a couple of campfires. The Americans sang songs of the Old West, led by the two gay dustmen from New York who were the only ones who knew all the words. We drank warming spirits from tin mugs. Og was nowhere to be seen, having retired to her tent as soon as the meal had been dished up.

Then she appeared from the shadows, shoving me roughly to one side in order to sit next to Steve. She smiled up at him, squeezing his arm in friendly fashion. He removed his arm and turned away.

So she grabbed it harder, pulling him round to face her. She said something very serious to him, judging by her tone of voice and the look on her face, not to mention the reactions of the driver and his girlfriend.

Things were beginning to look ugly, though Og had clearly attempted a transformation. She had put on a fresh sweater, discarded the dungarees for a pair of jeans, and made an effort to tame her wild Icelandic hair. Steve began to look worried.

As well he might. As far as Og was concerned, rejection was not an option.

There was a lot of Icelandic muttering from Og. We drew back a little from her and the helpless, hapless Steve. Now was definitely not the time to come between man and mate. Nor the time to curb the urges of Og.

After a few moments she dragged him, literally, from the fireside and into one of our tents. She was, as I mentioned, a hefty lass and Steve was powerless. After a moment, the side of the tent began to billow and shake as the pair of them rolled around inside. Steve's face appeared for a brief moment at the tent flap, his expression a mixture of desperation and pleading.

For a long time it was like something from a Tom and Jerry cartoon. The canvas billowing, the tent poles shivering and Steve's head and shoulders appearing intermittently before being dragged back inside by the girl he had planned only to trifle with – but who was determined to get what she wanted. Her just desserts, I suppose.

After a while, things quietened down. Tom, Robin, Roy and I managed to squeeze into our second tent, but we could not get a wink of sleep. For laughing.

We were due to fly back to Reykjavik the following day, which was just as well, considering the atmosphere that had been generated by the previous night's roistering. The Americans and the tour guide weren't too happy, but the driver, his girlfriend and Og were extremely displeased. Steve had caused great offence by his resistance to her charms. After a silent breakfast – Cornflakes in a hurricane again – we packed up the camp and set off for the airstrip.

The driver put on speed and seemed to seek out the roughest patches of a very rough road with fierce deliberation. Every time we banged and bounced around he turned to glare at us and snarl.

Og said little. And what she did say she said to the other girl, with many dark glances at Steve. It seemed he had added insult to injury by failing to come up to scratch in all departments.

When we reached the airstrip they pitched our gear and rucksacks on to the roadside and sped off in a storm of dust and small pebbles. No parting handshakes. No formal farewells. No surprise, really.

We were alone in a dark and dreary landscape. The rock and shale slopes rising from either side of the track were black and grey. The airstrip running beside the road was of crushed volcanic ash and shingle – black and grey again. The only spot of colour in the entire scene was the Dayglo orange windsock about half way along the strip. There was not a breath of wind, so it hung, limp, from its pole.

We all looked at it for a moment. Then, without exchanging a word, we all turned and looked at Steve.

It began to rain, so we gathered our metal boxes together and opened the big black umbrella that comes as part of the camera kit. Sitting on the boxes, the rain drumming remorselessly on the umbrella, our spirits began to sink.

'What time was the plane supposed to pick us up?' I asked Tom.

'They said around two o'clock', he replied.

'It's well after three,' said Robin.

'We could all die of hypothermia,' said Roy.

'I couldn't give a stuff,' said Steve.

Another rain-soaked hour passed. I was about to suggest writing messages to our loved ones on pages torn from my notebook which would be found on our bodies, when Robin said he could hear the sound of a plane.

Soon we all heard and saw it. A little dot approaching from above a line of distant hills. The dot became a plane which landed on the strip and taxied over to where we waited.

Killing the engine and climbing from the plane, the pilot apologised for the delay, explaining that he had a head cold and wasn't supposed to be flying, but could not get another pilot to take the job. The futile search for a substitute was the reason for his lateness.

We had, by now, almost forgotten about Og the Wench, apart from Steve who, let's face it, had more to remember than the rest of us. Instead we concentrated on loading our metal boxes and rucksacks into the little aircraft, and taking our seats. The pilot revved the engine and released the brakes. We did not move. Our total weight had caused the rear wheel to sink deep into the cinder surface of the strip.

So we got out, shifted the gear to the front of the cabin, and stood beside the plane as the pilot re-started the engine and slowly eased forward.

As it crept along, Tom clambered on board, followed by Roy and Steve. The plane gathered speed. Robin was hauled on board and finally I also made it, running along as fast as I could and flinging myself at the open door and the outstretched arms of my fellow travellers.

The door was heaved shut and locked as we rose from the end of the airstrip and headed for Reykjavik. The pilot flew as low as he safely could, because of the pressure on his ears, but as we sped towards Reykjavik the terrain rose and thick black clouds dropped to meet it. The horizontal strip of clear sky ahead became narrower and narrower. It was genuinely frightening, and I hate to think of the discomfort our pilot must have been suffering.

But a little under an hour later, we landed safely. Prudence and Ted were waiting with a minibus.

'Did everything go as planned?' she asked.

'Oh, pretty much,' replied Tom.

'No problems at all?' asked Ted, with, I thought, a touch of disappointment in his voice.

'Nothing worth mentioning,' said Tom.

The rest of us stayed silent. But, as we hauled the gear into the minibus I couldn't help wondering whether I would go on more filming trips – and if so, how many of them would involve 'nothing worth mentioning'.

Afterword

I've got to stop now because my wrists and fingers are aching from all the typing. And because what I have written should have been handed over to the good folk at Bradt this morning.

Travel writers – all writers, come to that – have to work to deadlines, whether producing an article for a newspaper or magazine, a commentary or script for a television report, or a book. Otherwise, the system falls apart and nothing would ever be published.

My life has been a succession of deadlines, and I have learned that the worst thing an editor can do is give people like me plenty of time to complete their task.

Tell us you want 2,000 words by three o'clock this afternoon and, grumbling heartily, we'll buckle down to it and deliver the goods.

Tell us you won't need those 2,000 words until a week next Thursday and we'll find masses of other things to do until ten o'clock in the morning of a week next Thursday.

'Never give a journalist time,' somebody once told me. 'They'll only waste it.' How true.

So I now realise I have reached the deadline without telling you about Chalkie the ten-dollar dove, and how he came to fly from a stall in an Orlando flea market to a custom-built residence in my back garden here in southeast London.

I haven't told you about my encounter with Mr Poppleton or Mr Popovic. The former was the last Englishman to be a game ranger in

Uganda; the latter one of the assassins who knocked off Archduke Franz Ferdinand in Sarajevo in 1914 and started the First World War.

I haven't got around to a stack of tales from Ireland or Alaska. Nor given you the grisly details of what happened when I went with my son (and the rest of his Cub Scout pack) on a 'lads and dads' bonding weekend under canvas. That last may not be the most exotic of my experiences away from home, but it is seared in my memory.

There's also the story of the Useless Information Society, and how I qualified for membership at the behest of David Ash.

Not to mention another selection of stories from Australia, or the time we tangled with authority in the Seychelles. As for that first trip to Brunei, well words would fail me if I didn't do words for a living.

So those stories – and a few more – will have to be told at some future date. Thank goodness I don't have a deadline...

Acknowledgements

I am particularly grateful to Jennifer Barclay, who has edited my work most sympathetically, and whose constructive criticism saved me from making a complete ass of myself in respect of one story. Thanks also for their support and encouragement to the team at Bradt, for whom this represents a significant departure from their norm.

I couldn't have travelled the world as I did without the understanding and support of my family. After 48 years of marriage, Sheila died in 2007, but she knew how much I loved and depended on her. Susan, Sarah and Matthew are now grown up with children of their own (and, in Susan's case, grandchildren too). They are three of the finest people I know. The jury is still out as to whether this is despite, or because of, my absences.

Finally, special thanks to Carole Howkins, who came into my life in 2009, made it better, and persuaded me to write down what would otherwise have remained half-forgotten, after-dinner anecdotes.